THE OPPOSITE SEX
BY Viv Quillin

GRAFTON BOOKS

A Division of the Collins Publishing Group

LONDON GLASGOW
TORONTO SYDNEY AUCKLAND

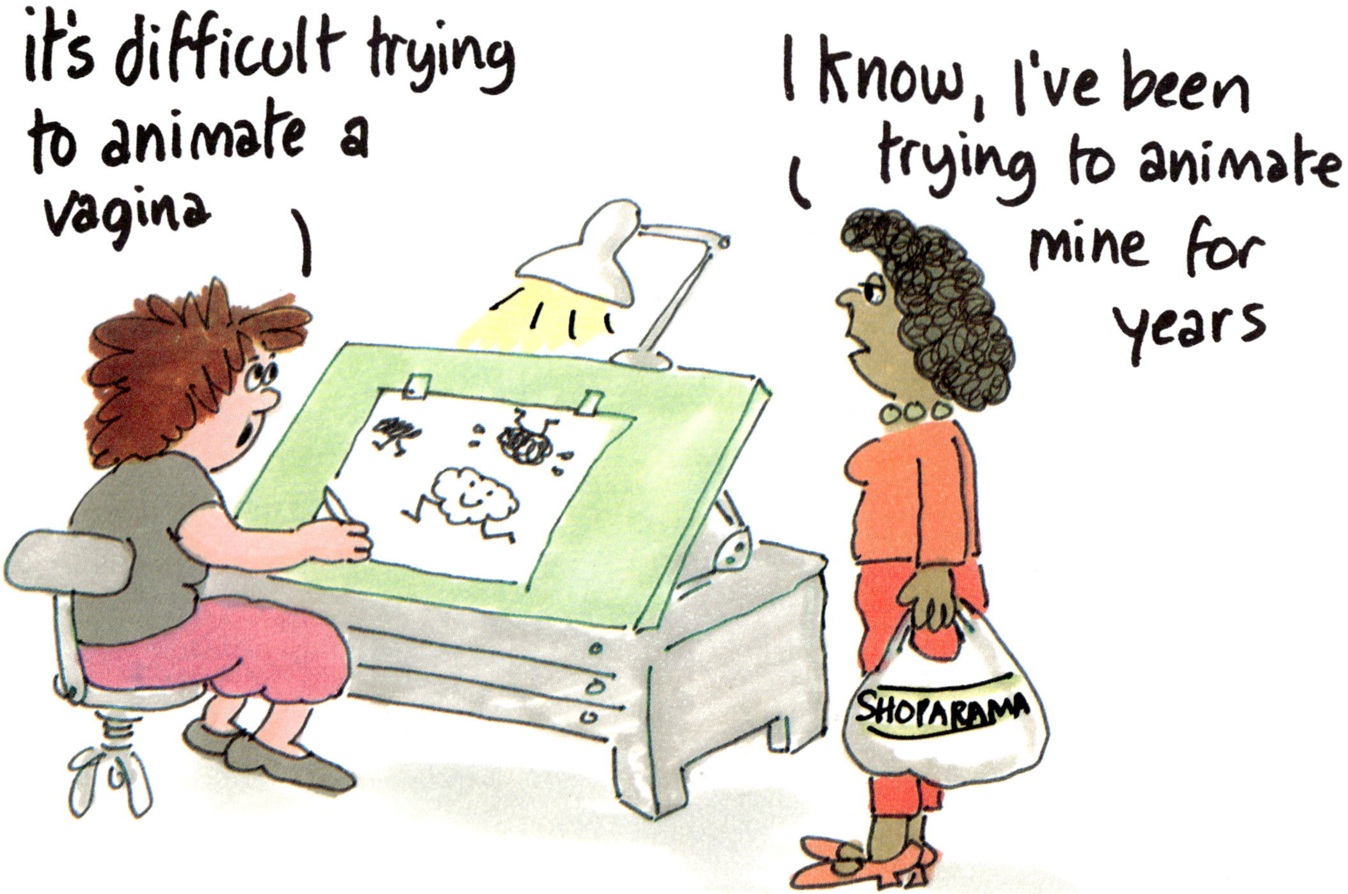
it's difficult trying to animate a vagina
I know, I've been trying to animate mine for years
SHOPARAMA

INTRODUCTION

So much has been said about sex by male cartoonists, I feel some insights from a female point of view are long overdue.

Women's bodies are not here simply for the entertainment of fellas, we have our very own foibles, fantasies and faux pas to deal with.

I've always failed miserably in the multiple orgasm stakes (mother told me never to fiddle with things I didn't understand). This leaves me suitably experienced in the 'well she tries hard' category, to describe many aspects of *Down Below.*

Most women – as well as men – are totally mystified by what goes on behind those fur curtains. Now is your chance to find out!

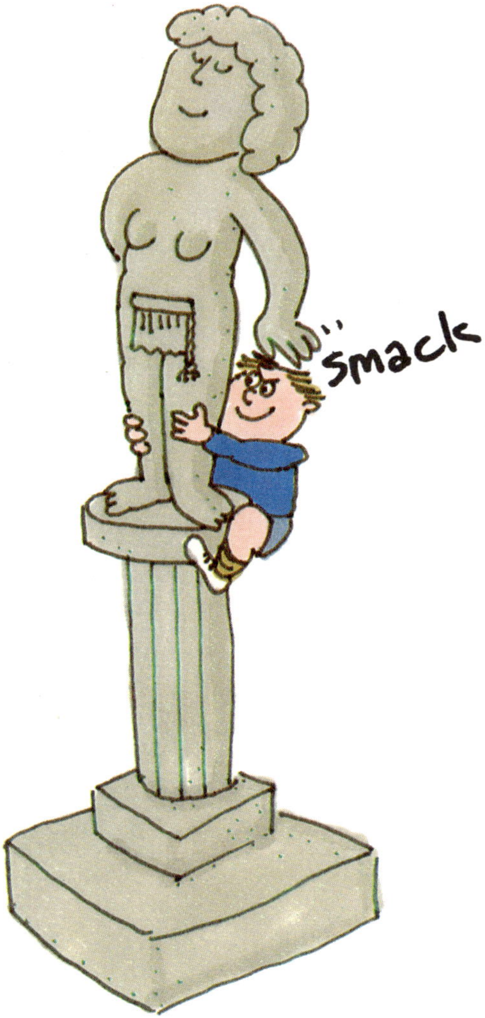
smack

THE BIG DIFFERENCE

Willies are pinned on the front, in clear view of their owners and any other interested parties . . .

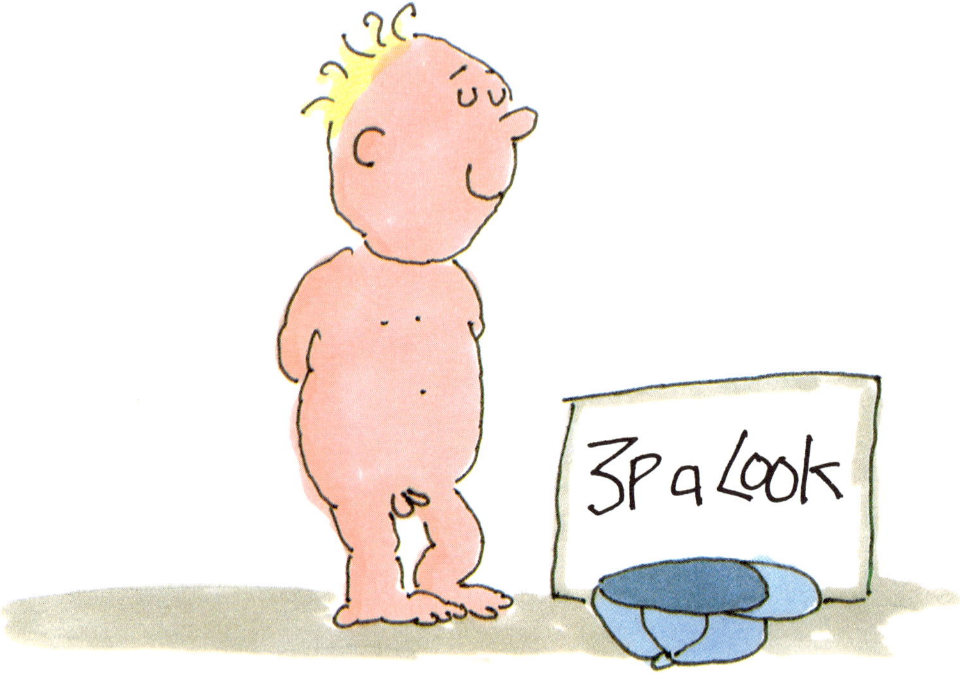
3P a Look

. . . but it takes a more dedicated genital spotter to see what a Vajee* looks like.

3P towards
FUNDING A
SEARCH PARTY

*Pronounced Văjee – abbreviated form of vagina. Vagina – part of woman's anatomy, otherwise known as Woman's Best Friend.

FOR WOMEN READERS WHO STILL AREN'T SURE

You are not a boy who
accidentally pulled a bit off.
Neither can you alter your size,
colour or chances of getting into
parliament, by what you and
Snowdrop The Fluffy Panda got
up to, when you were seven.

You'll go blind ⟶

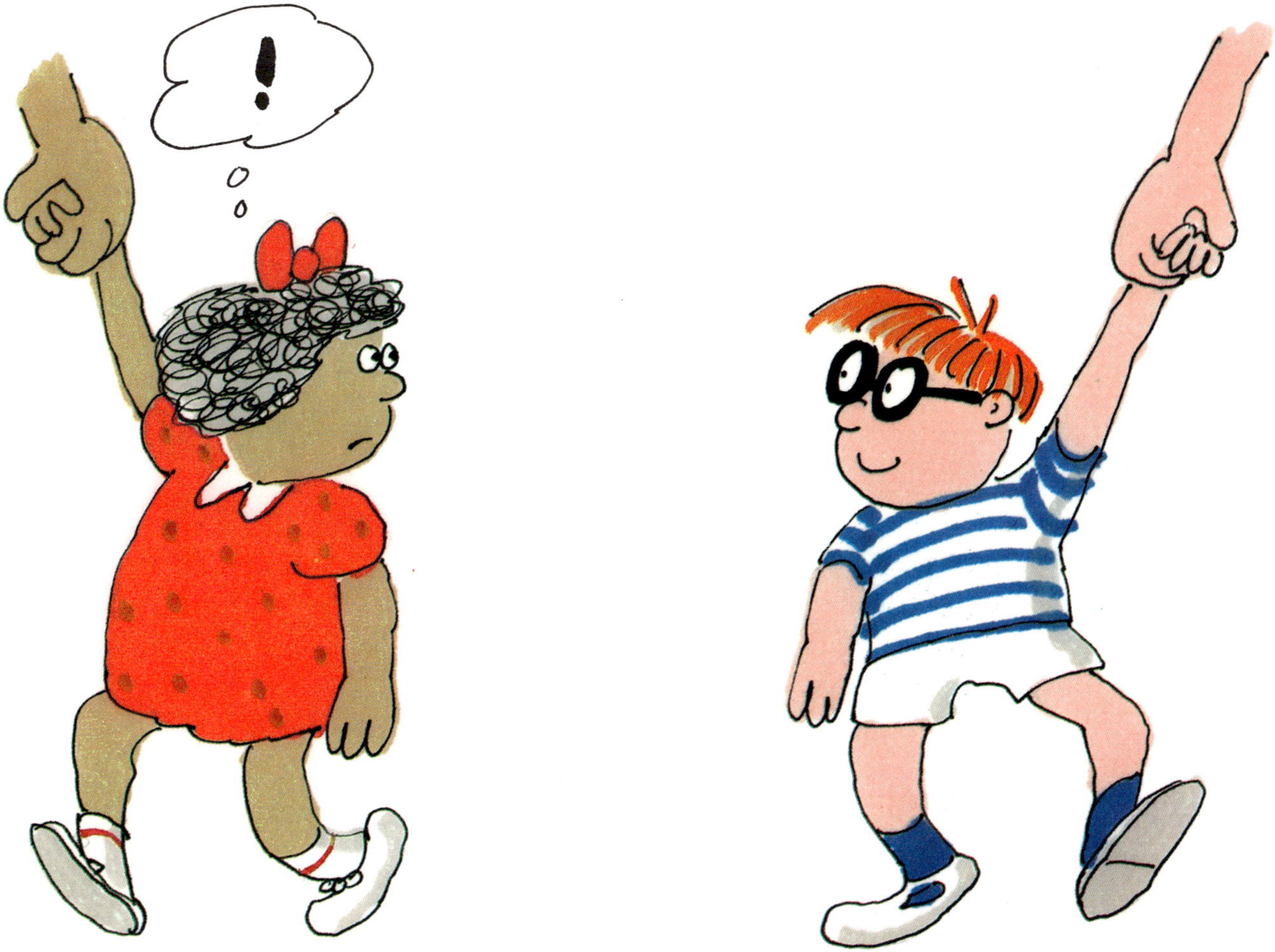
!

SEX EDUCATION AT HOME

Basically, little boys are expected to be naughty, dirty and rude (this includes sex).

Little girls are expected to be *nice* (this doesn't include sex).

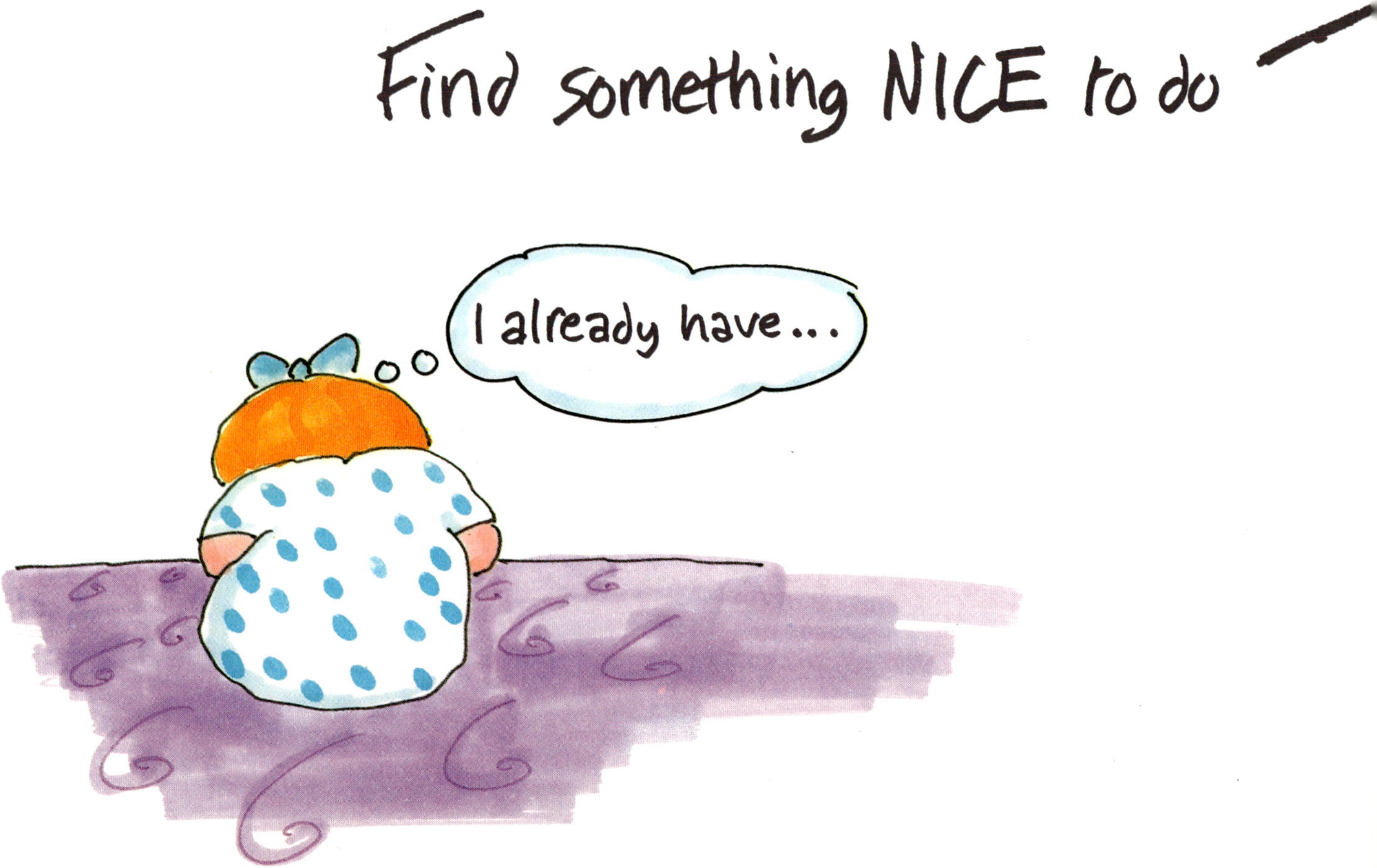

Find something NICE to do
I already have...

SEX EDUCATION AT SCHOOL

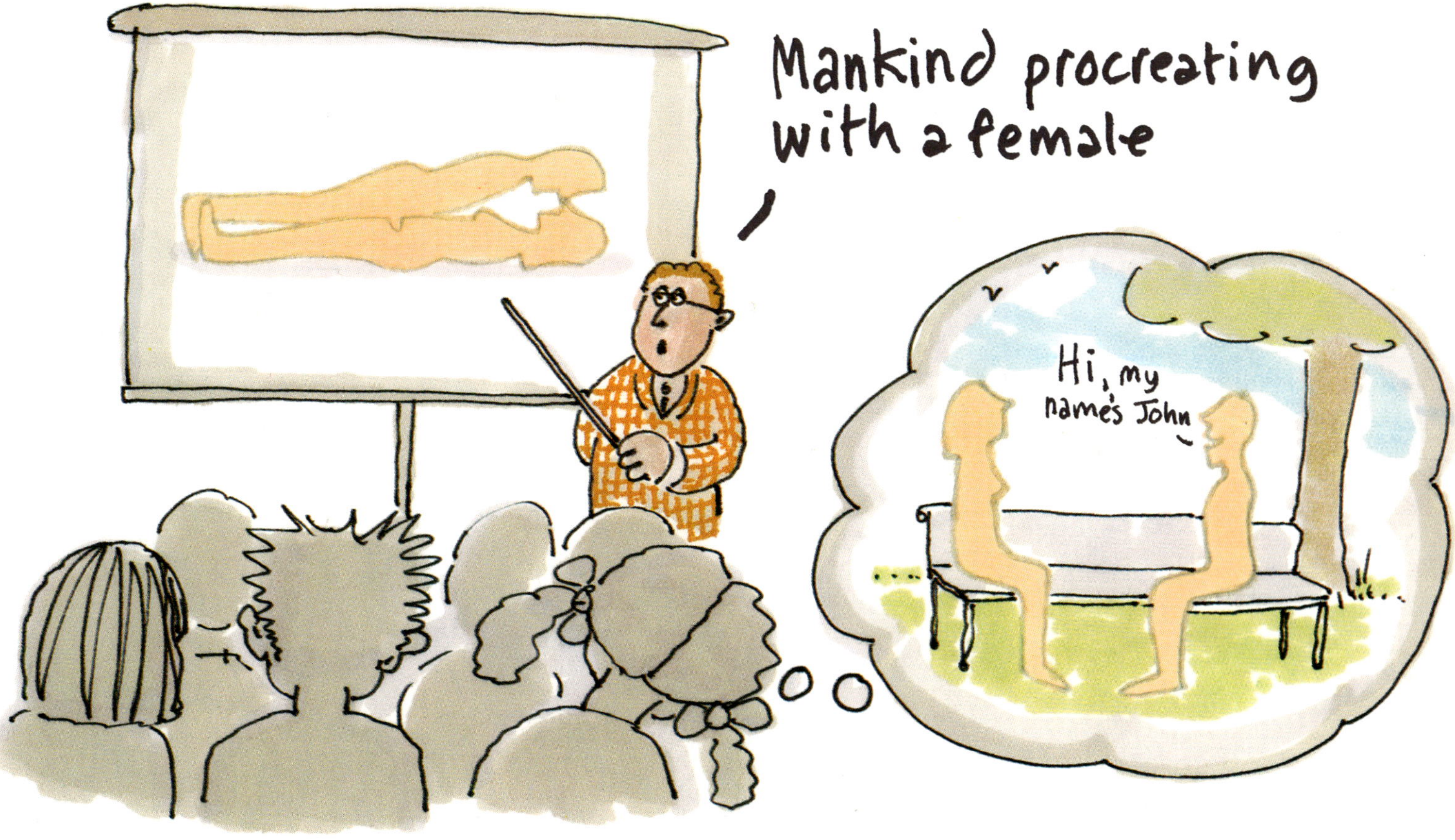
Mankind procreating with a female
Hi, my name's John

GROWING UP
(and sideways and forwards).

Followed very quickly by *menstruation.*

Now is the time for a girl to receive some motherly advice . . .

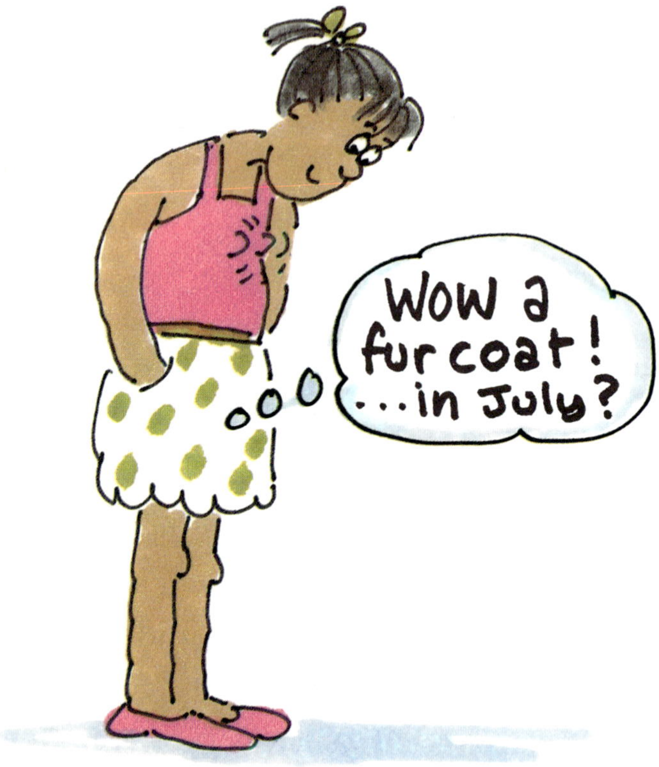
Wow a fur coat! ...in July?

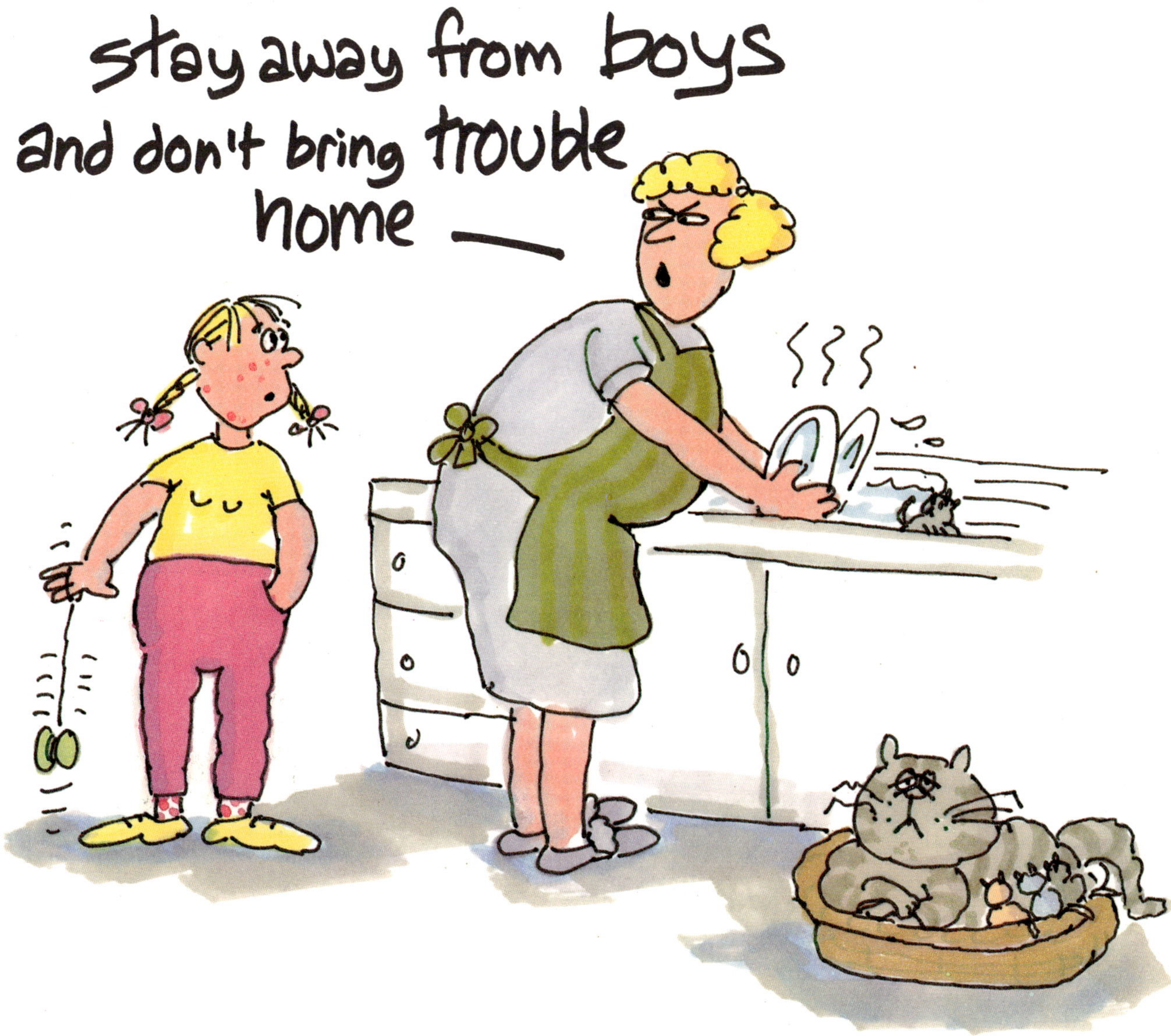
stay away from boys
and don't bring trouble
home —

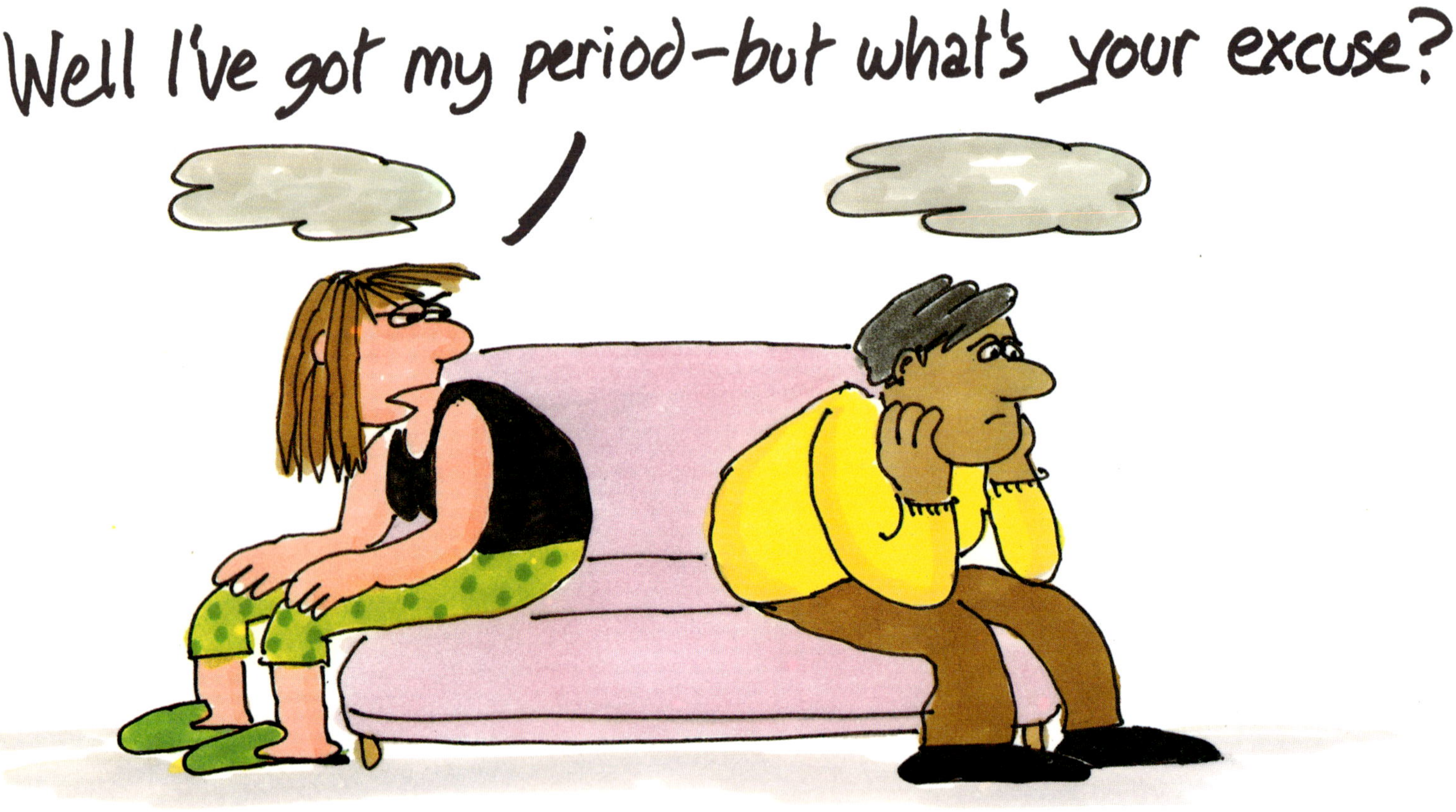
Well I've got my period–but what's your excuse?

THE REDS ARE COMING!

Advanced technology caters for every woman's needs, from the Teeny Tampette to the Giant Super Plus Pad which doubles as a sleeping bag.

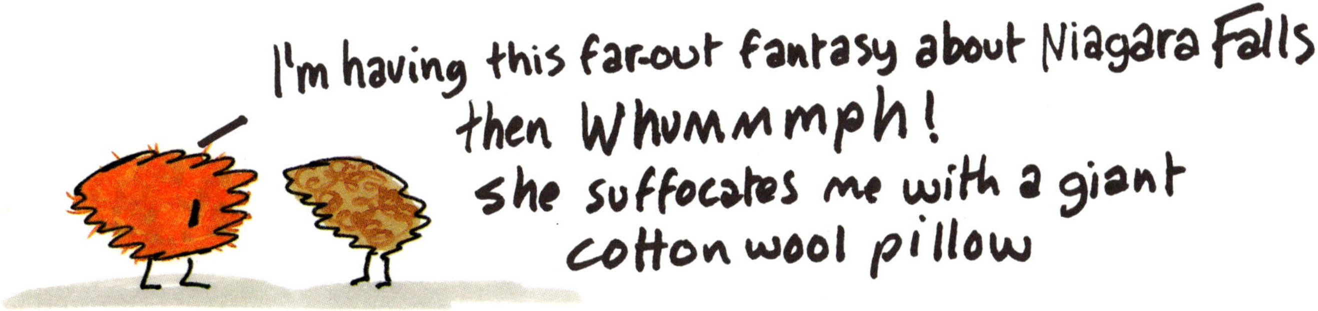
I'm having this far-out fantasy about Niagara Falls
then Whummmph!
she suffocates me with a giant
cotton wool pillow

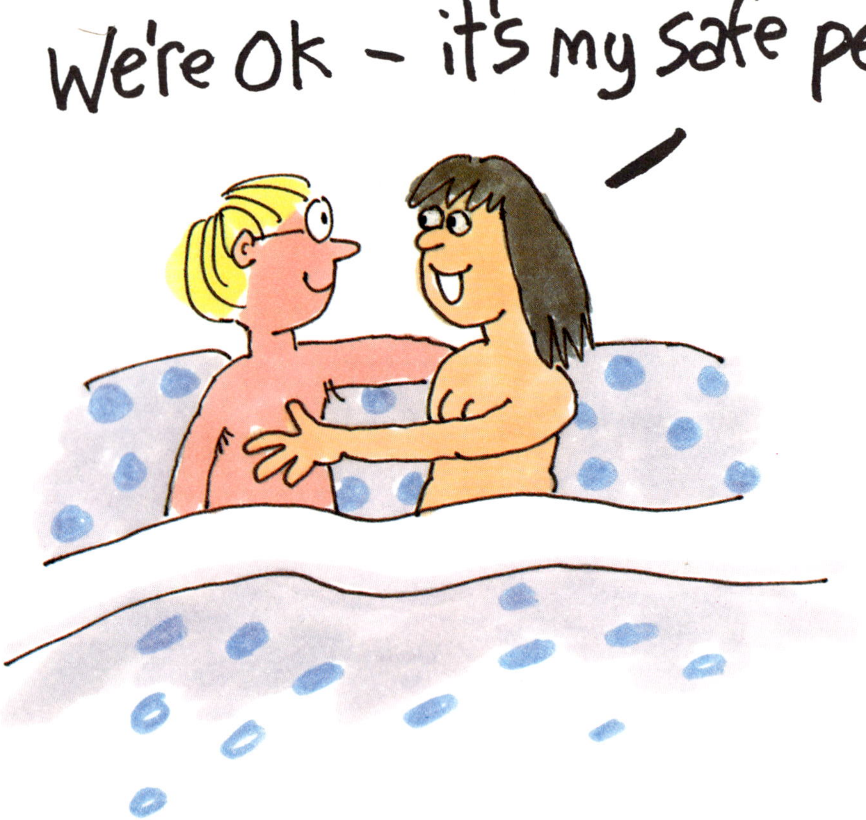
We're OK – it's my safe period

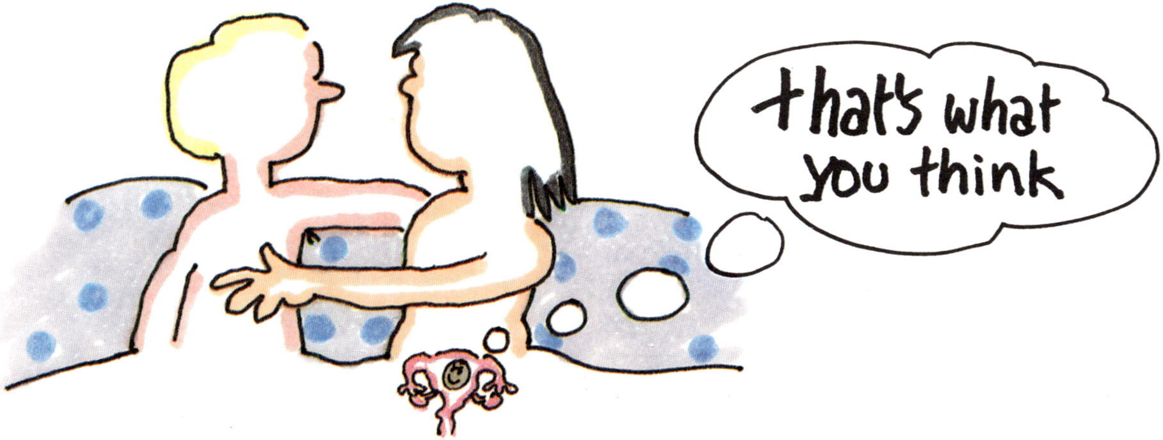
that's what you think

FEMALE ANATOMY

Includes centrally heated nursery accommodation, totally redecorated every month, plus the usual plumbing fixtures.

It's not surprising that doctors connect up the wrong bits sometimes . . .

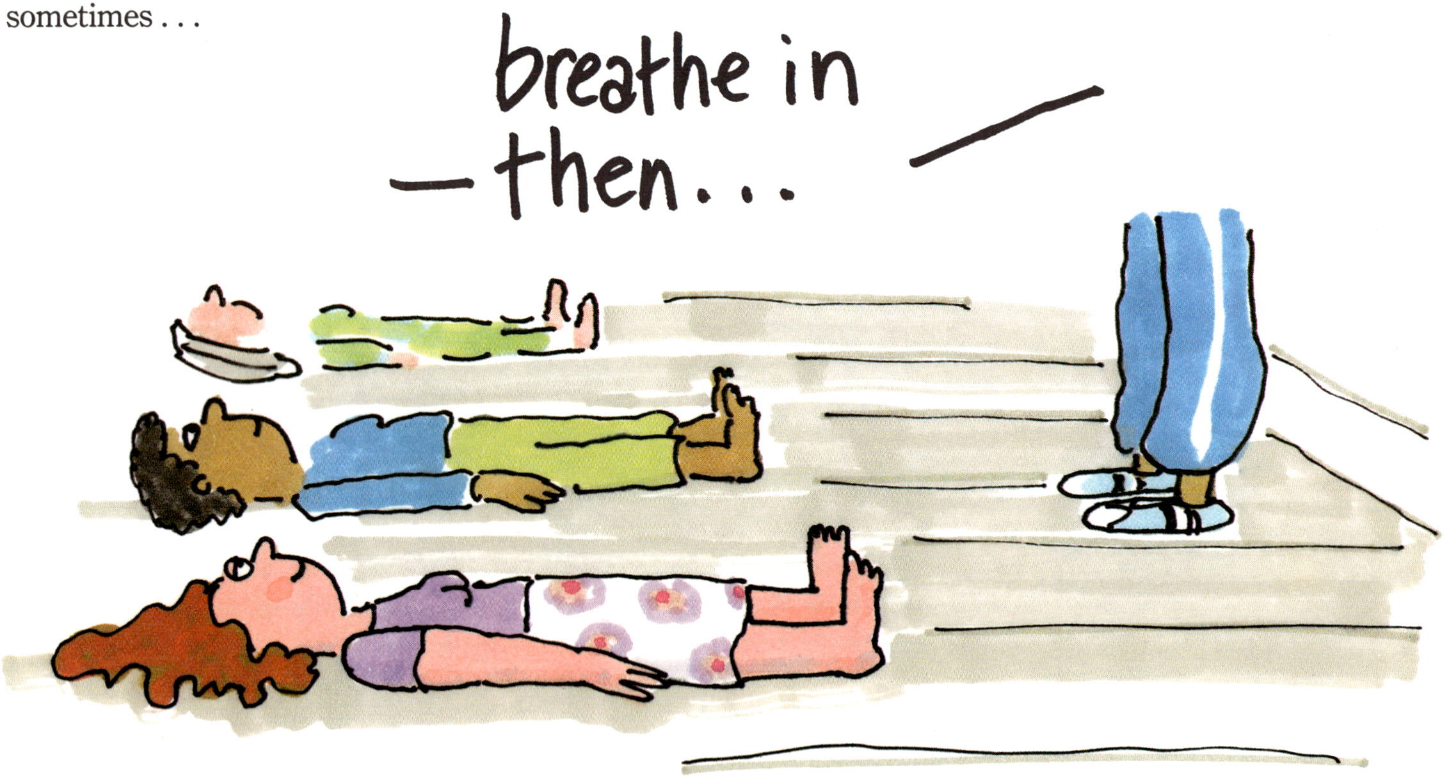
breathe in
— then. . .

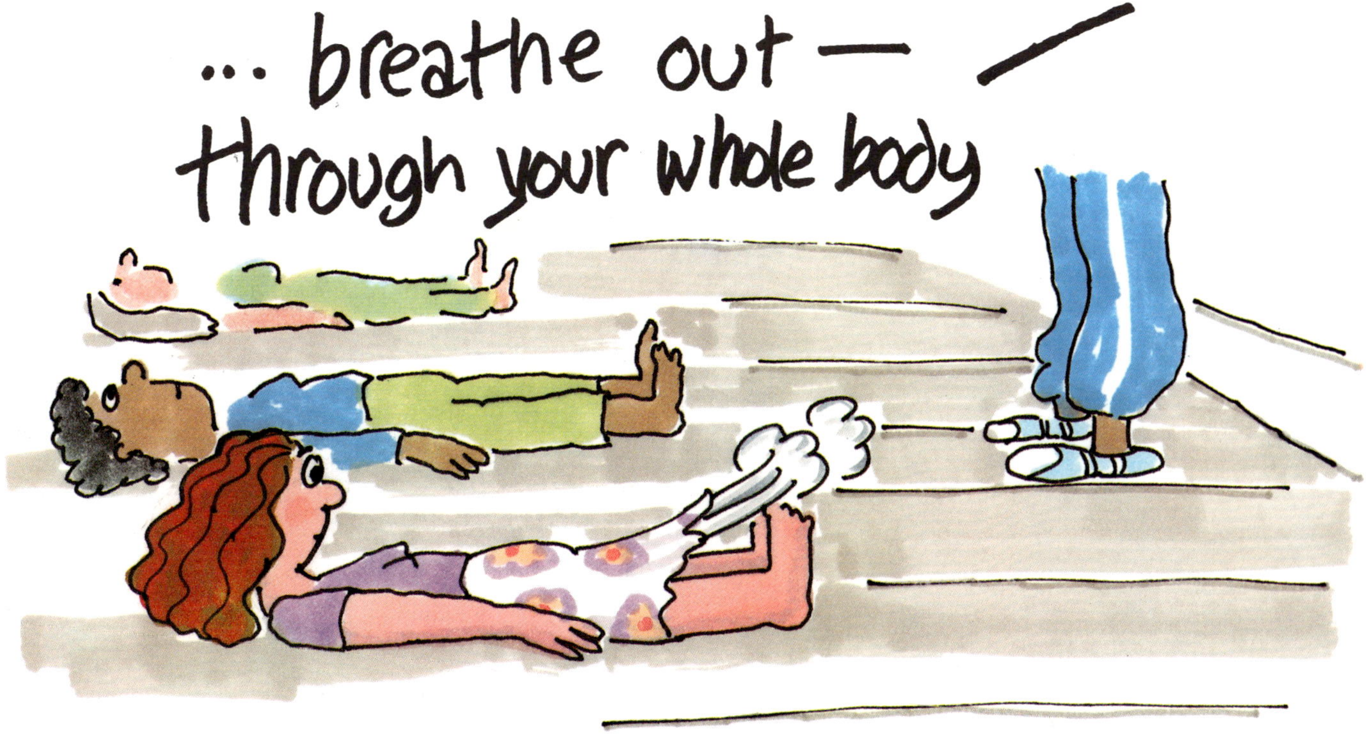
... breathe out — —
through your whole body

MEDICAL RESEARCH

Women have been known to insert a 'No Through Traffic' sign due to the number of medics eager to inspect their nether regions. She's only got to lie down in a hospital and a thousand spotty students file past like it's a state funeral.

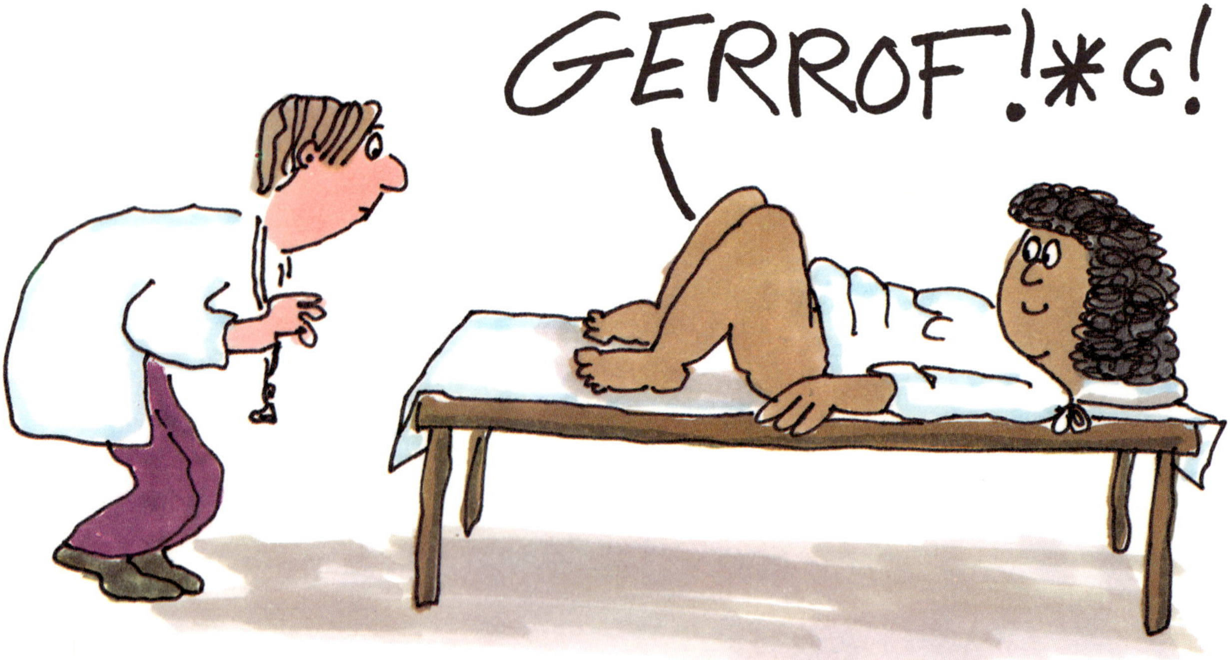
GERROF!*G!

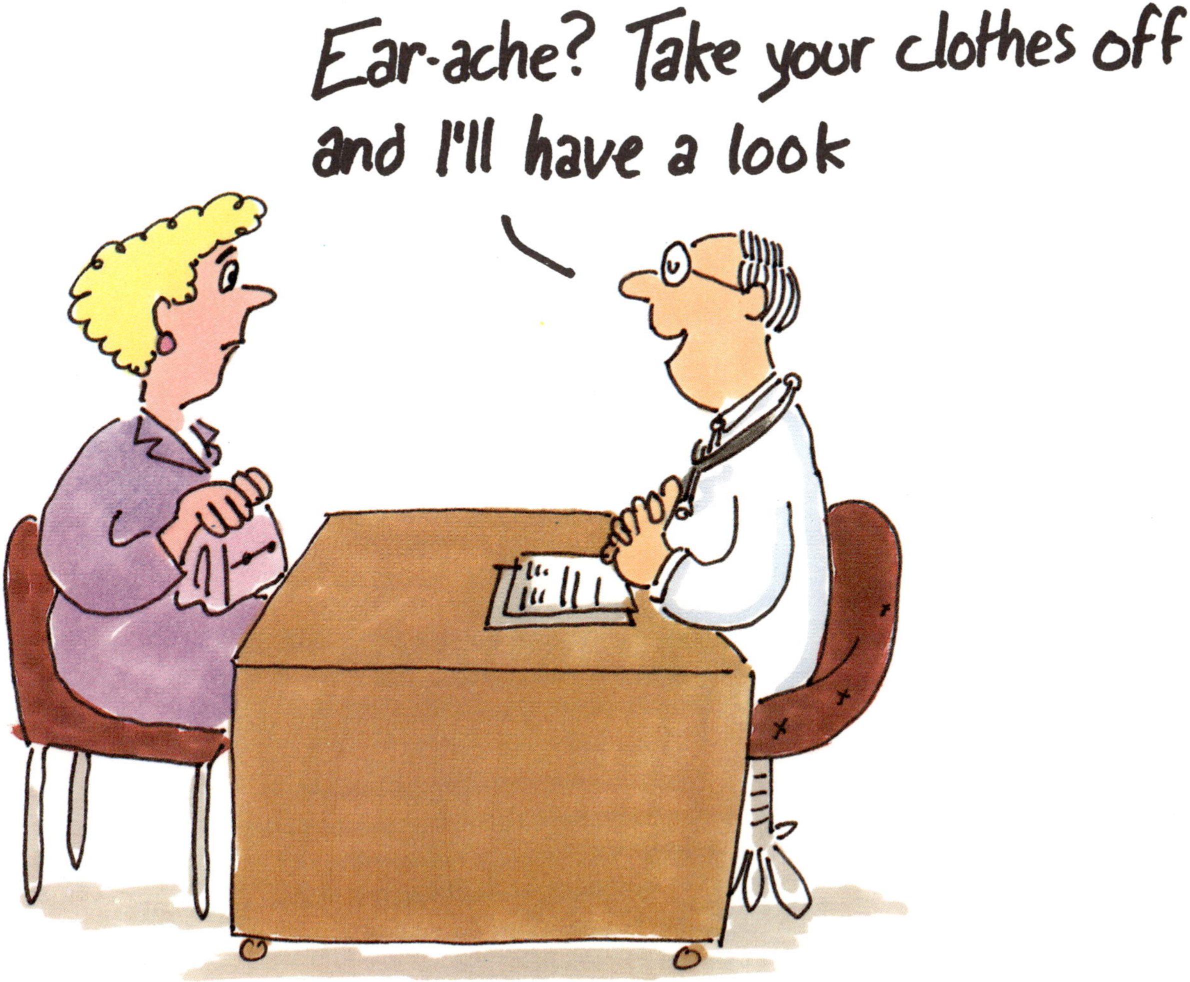
Ear-ache? Take your clothes off and I'll have a look

for those who wonder what goes on underneath...

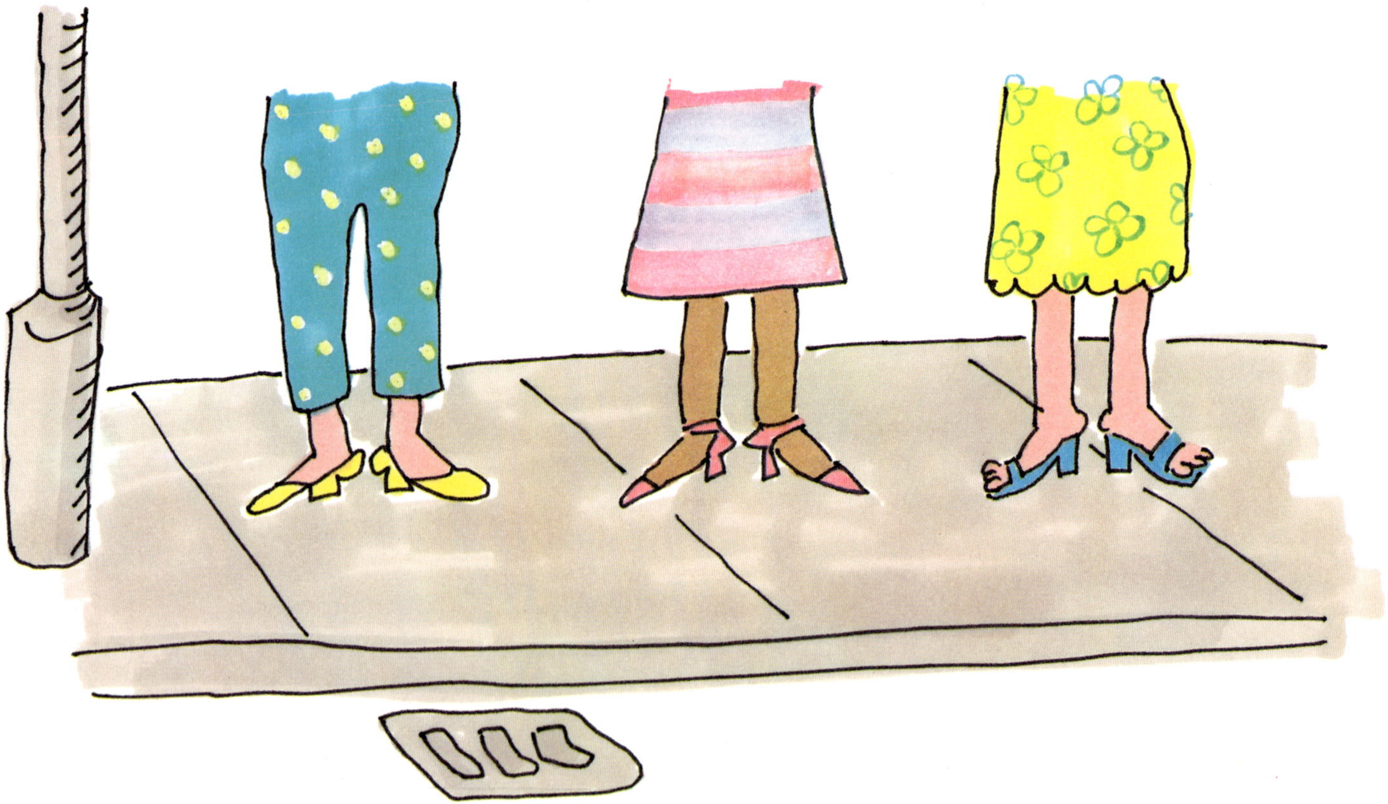

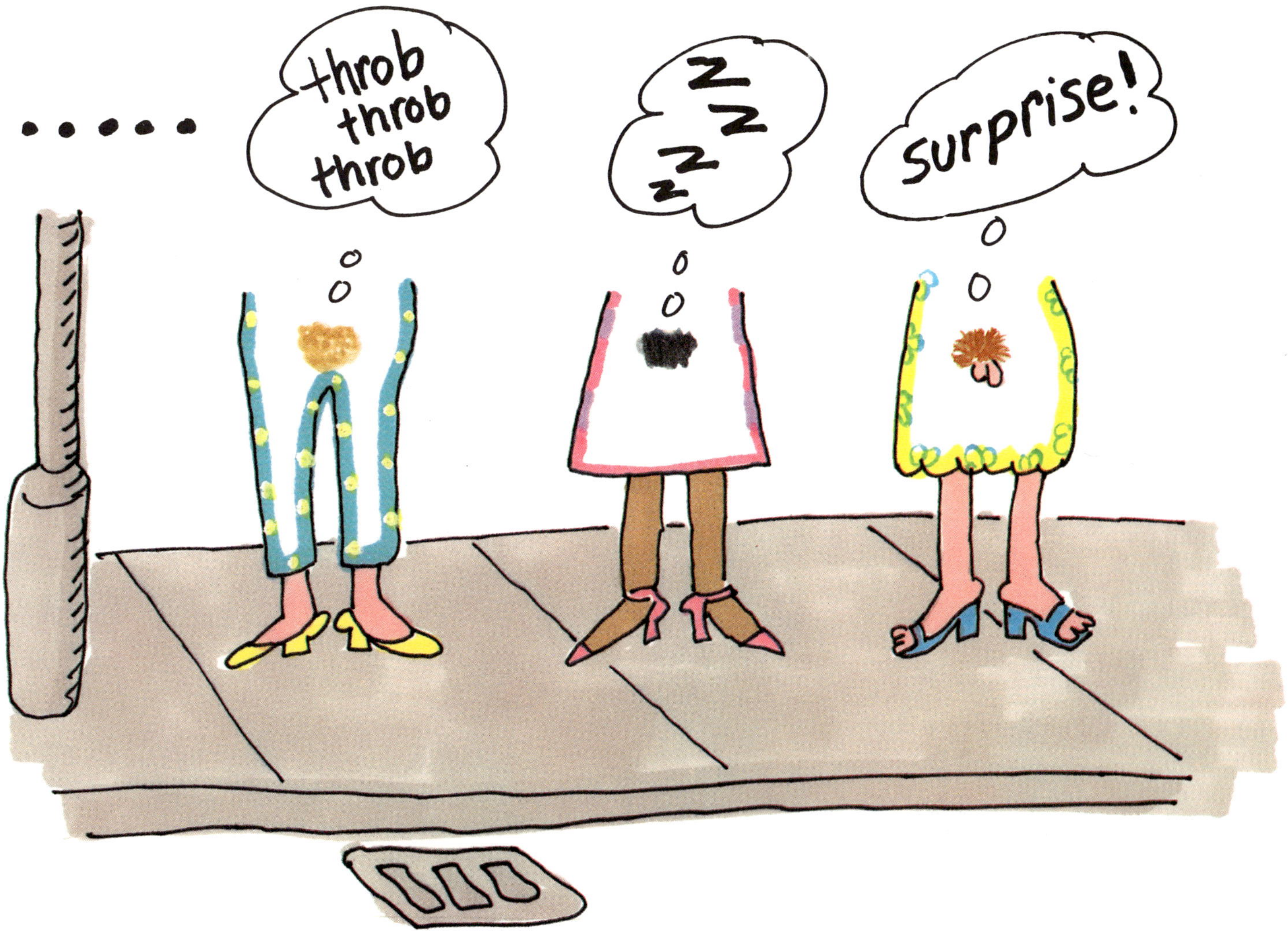

throb throb throb
z z z z
surprise!

POPULAR VAJEE MYTH

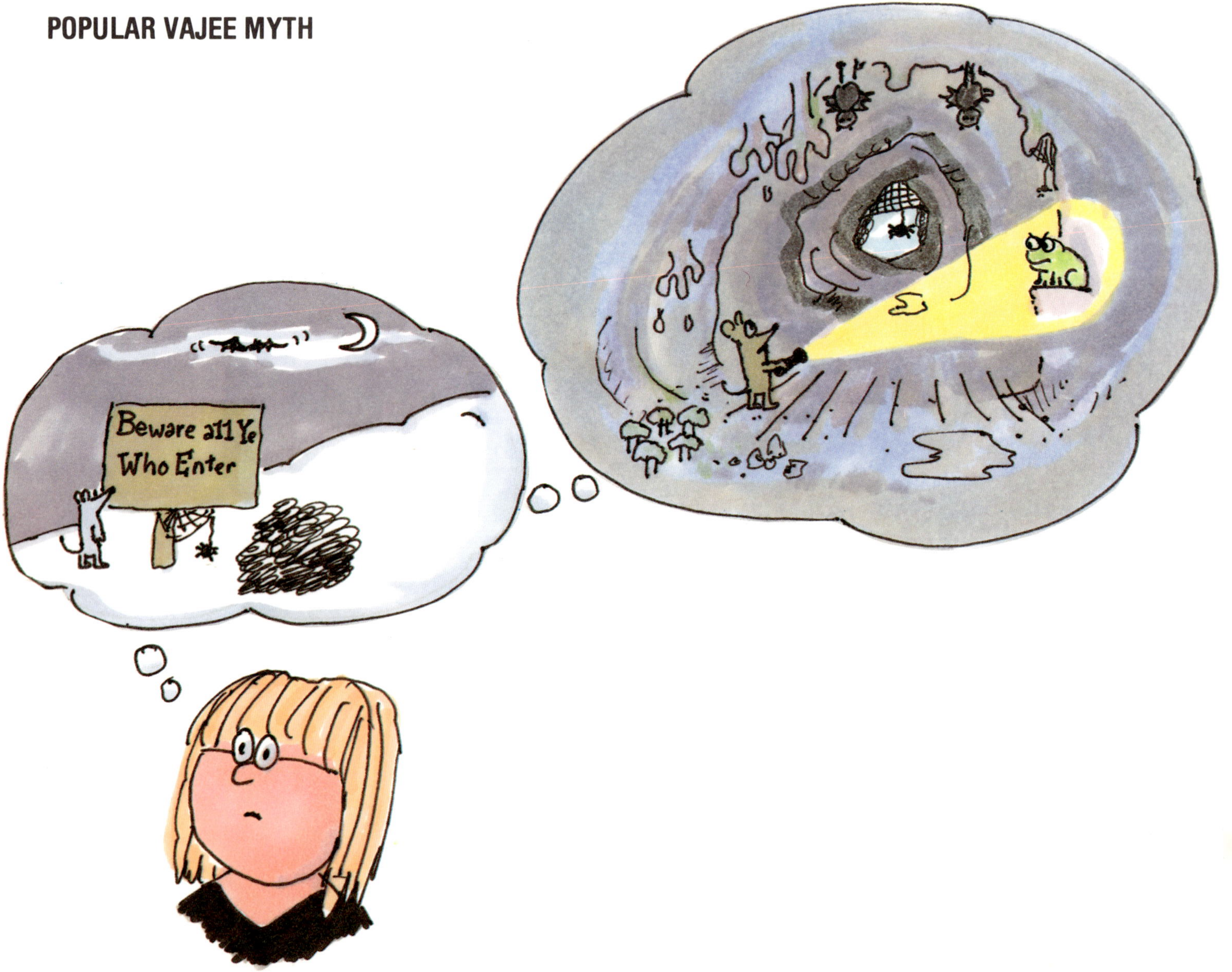

Beware all Ye
Who Enter

RECLAIMING THE RUDE BITS

This is often done in groups and can include exercises like talking to cushions, looking up *other women's,* and other things that most people would get locked up for.

All with a view to loving your Vajee without shame.

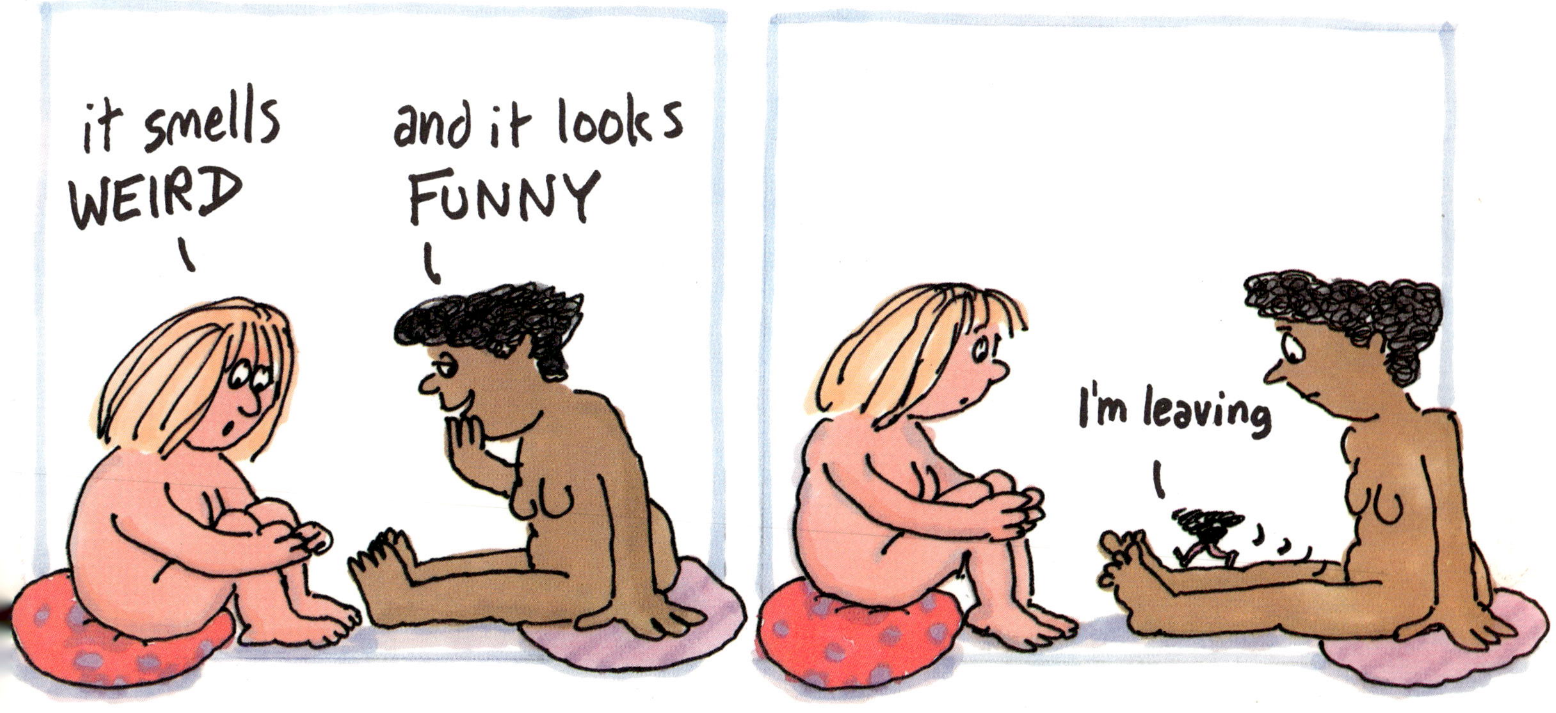
it smells WEIRD
and it looks FUNNY
I'm leaving

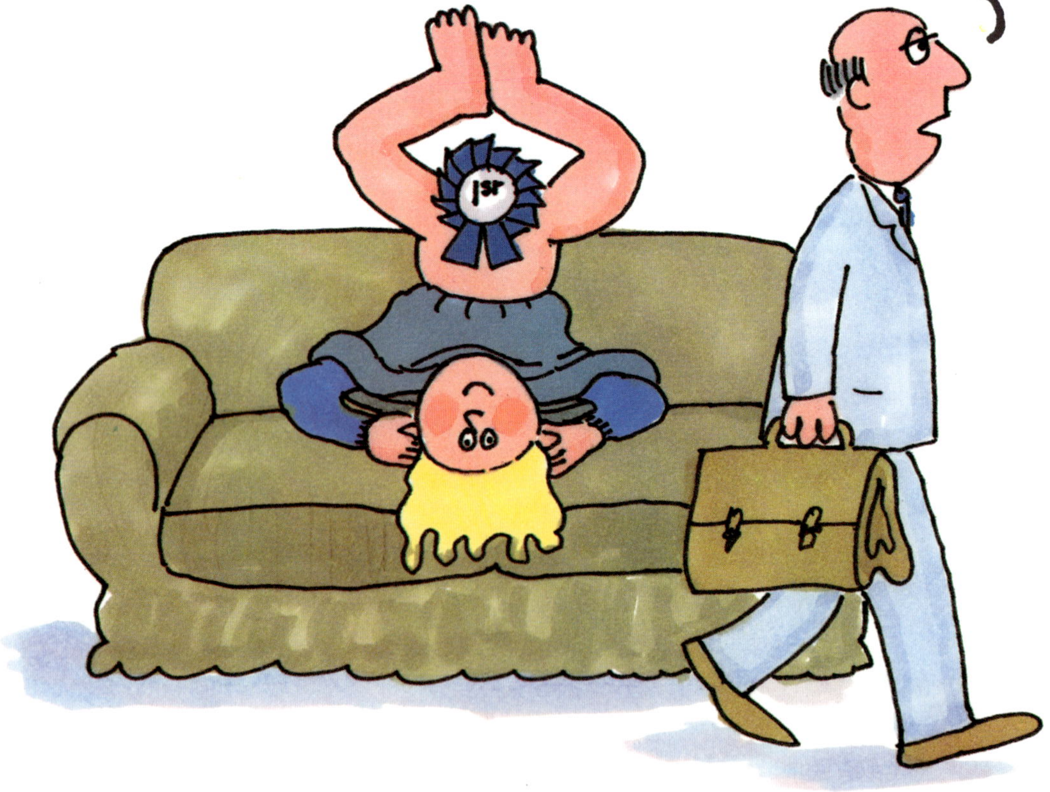
still reading "Love Me, Love My Genitals," Dear?

"Monica's been on this marvellous self-examination course"...

FIRST NIGHT NERVES

A good way of oiling the works is a total body massage, this gives you time to relax and get to know each other more. Particularly with the super, giant-size woman.

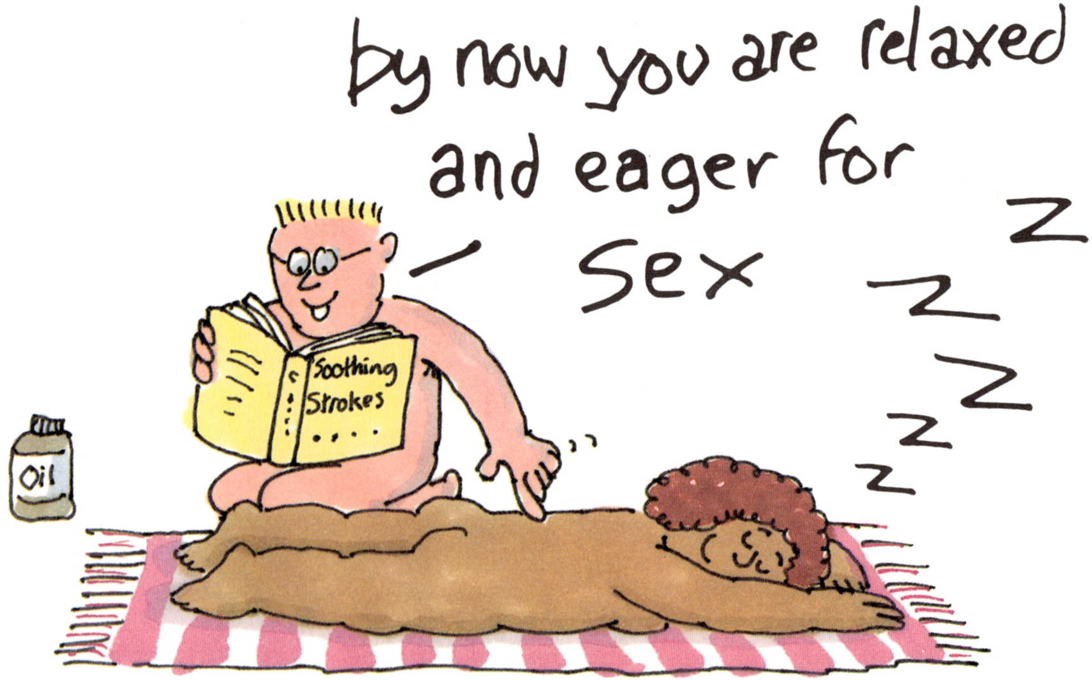
by now you are relaxed and eager for sex
Z Z Z Z Z
Soothing Strokes
Oil

PLEASURE ZONES – the H* Spot

Forget flowers and chocs. Most women can be reduced to a quivering mass of pleasure at the sight of someone else doing the housework.

(Listening to tapes of the vacuum cleaner running is *not* the same.)

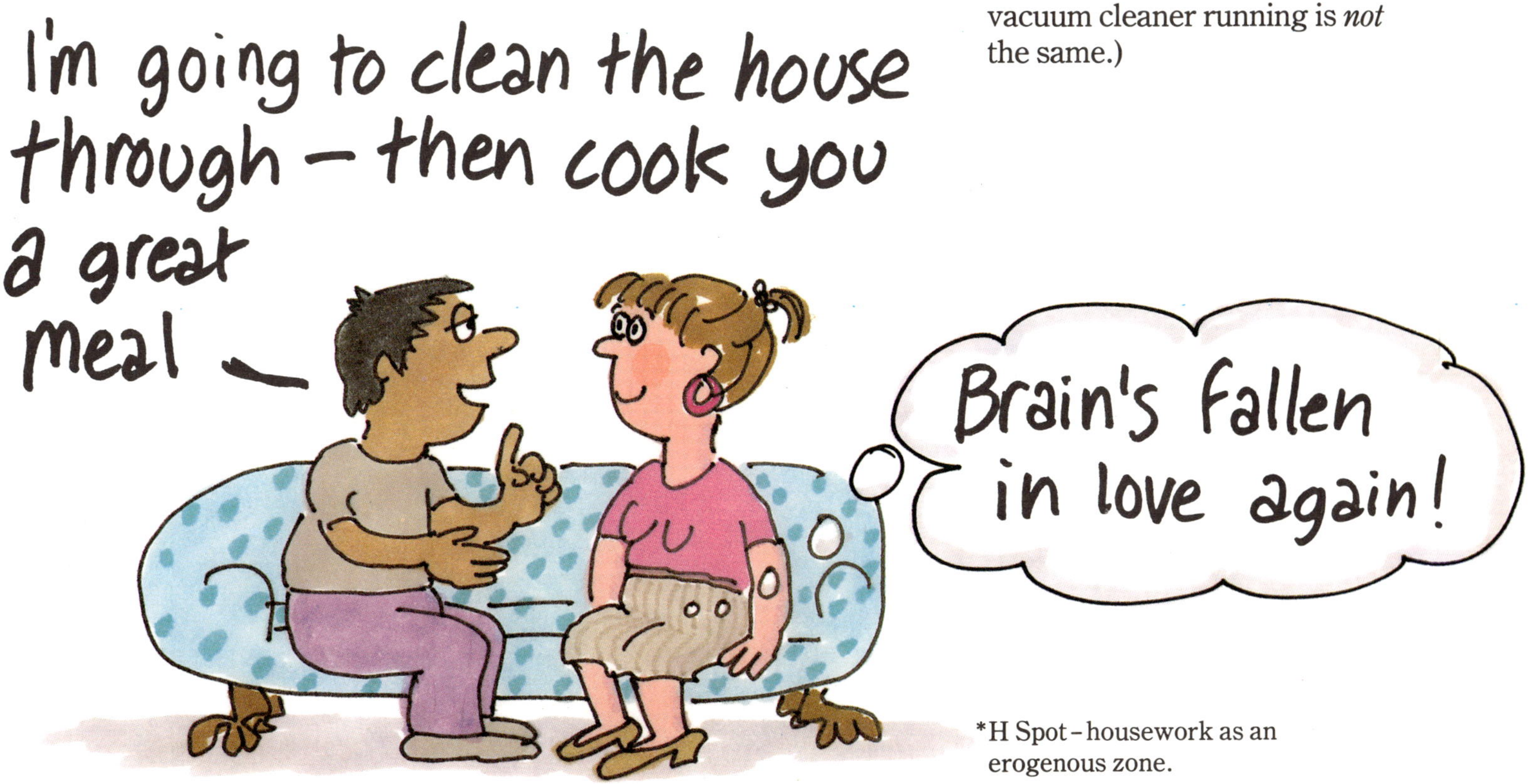
I'm going to clean the house through – then cook you a great meal
Brain's fallen in love again!

*H Spot – housework as an erogenous zone.

BEWARE . . .

of the guy who insists *all* women enjoy being pinched, pummelled or tweaked *there.* (Meaning the girl he practised on in Junior School, who didn't like to complain.)

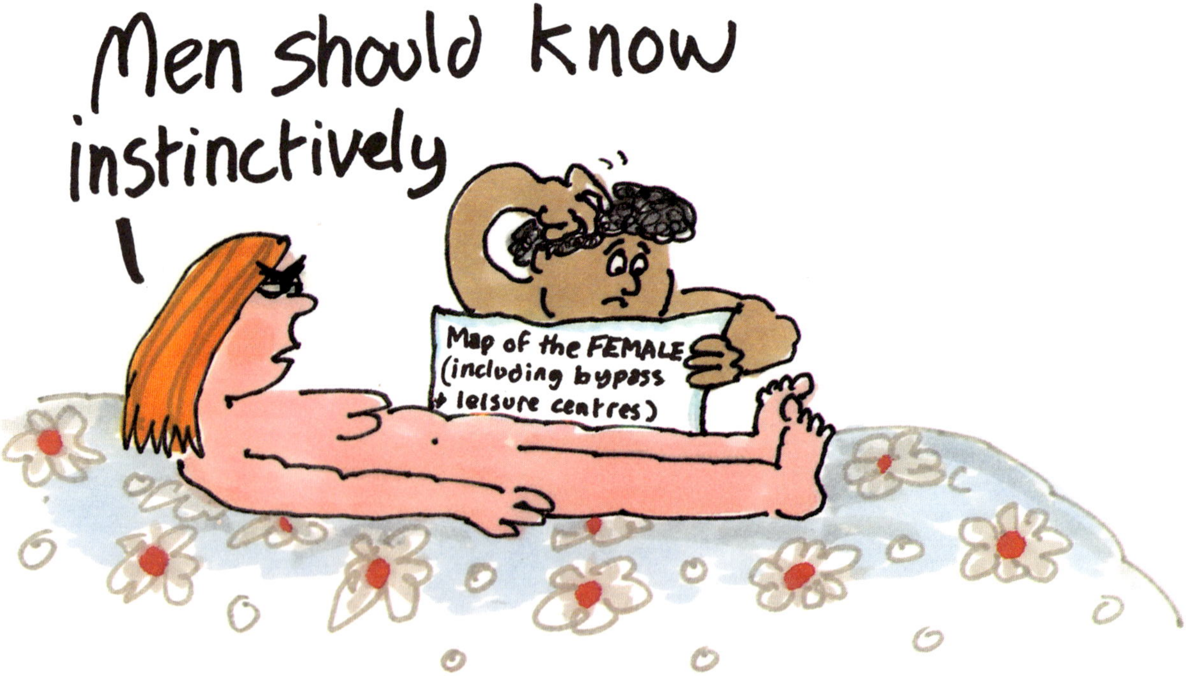
Men should know instinctively
Map of the FEMALE (including bypass + leisure centres)

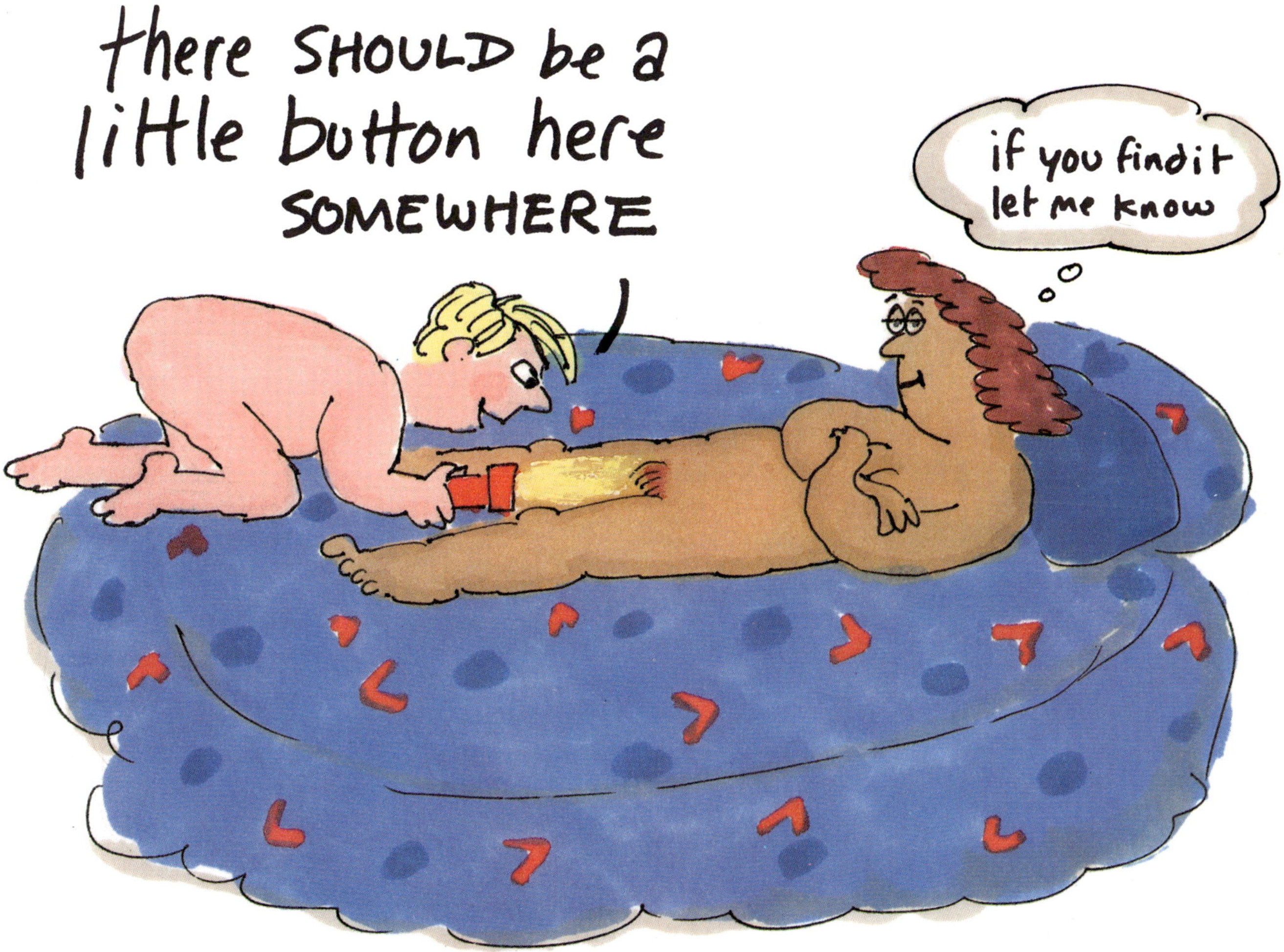
there SHOULD be a little button here SOMEWHERE
if you find it let me know

TECHNICAL SECTION – step by step guide to female orgasm

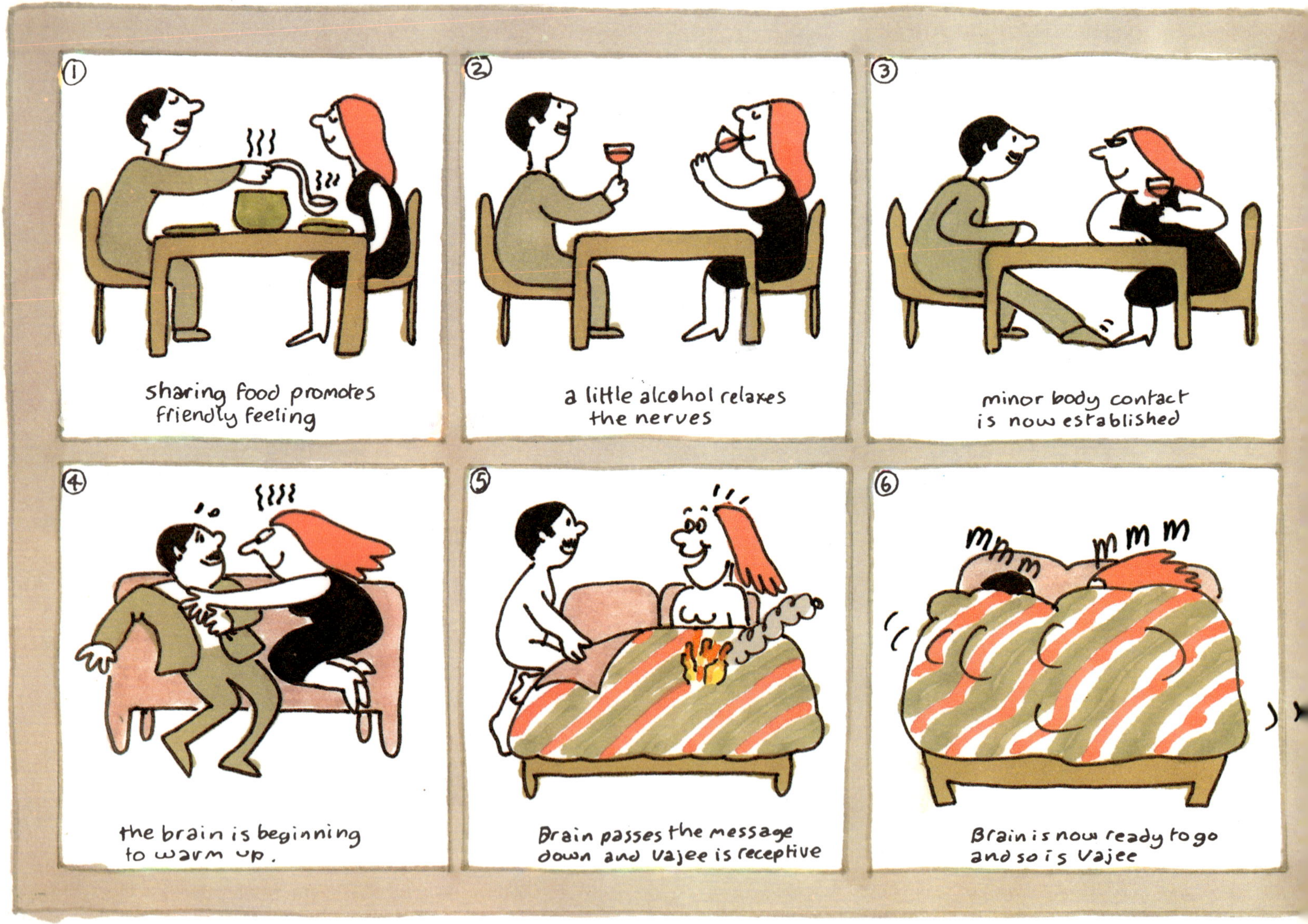

1
sharing food promotes friendly feeling
2
a little alcohol relaxes the nerves
3
minor body contact is now established
4
the brain is beginning to warm up.
5
Brain passes the message down and Vajee is receptive
6
mmm
mmm
Brain is now ready to go and so is Vajee

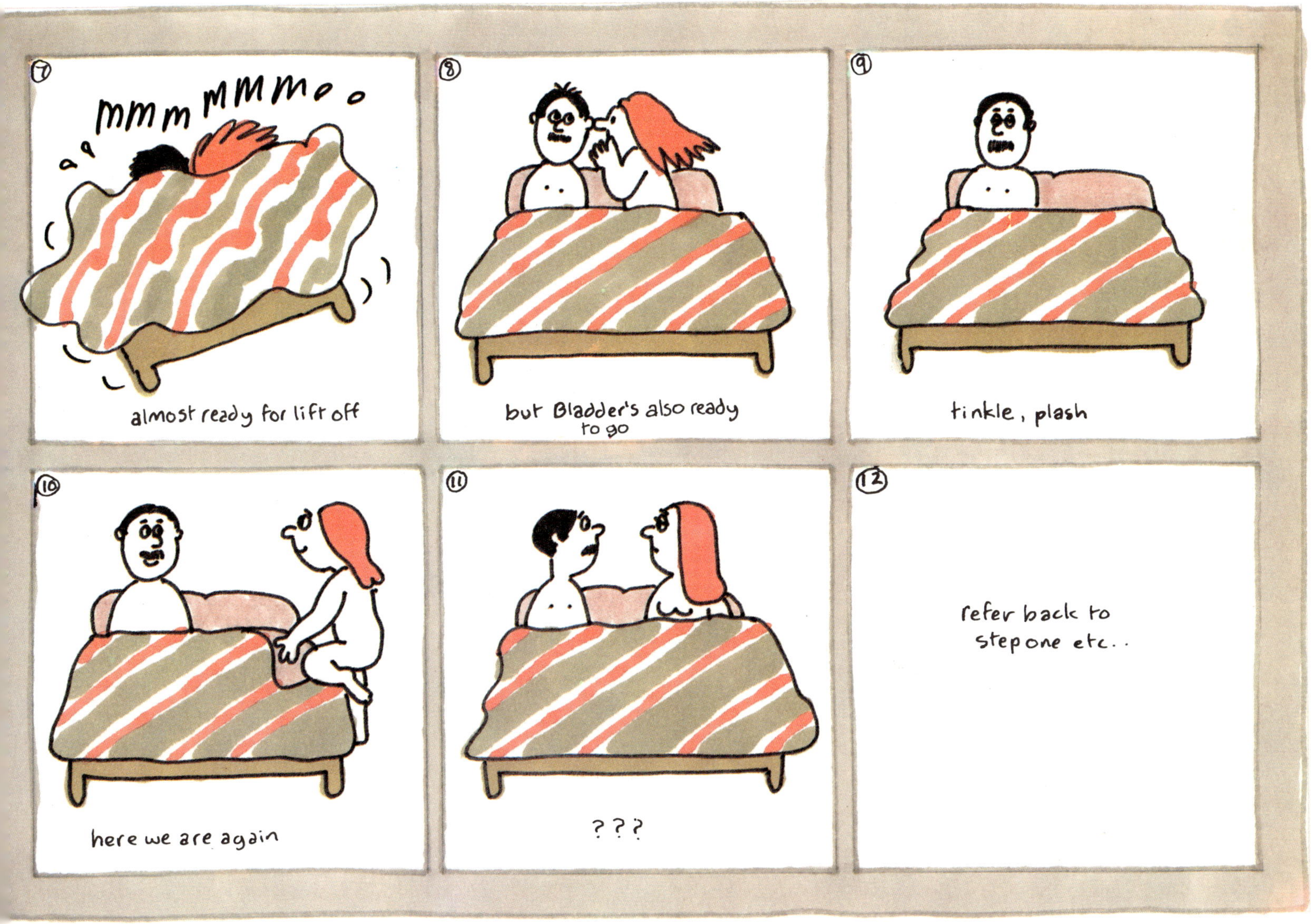
mmmmMMMmoo
almost ready for lift off
but Bladder's also ready to go
tinkle, plash
here we are again
???
refer back to step one etc..

THE BIG 'O'*

So far we don't have an Official Sexual Olympics, but it's only a matter of time. Enjoying yourself is no longer enough. Strict training and ruthless determination are required . . .

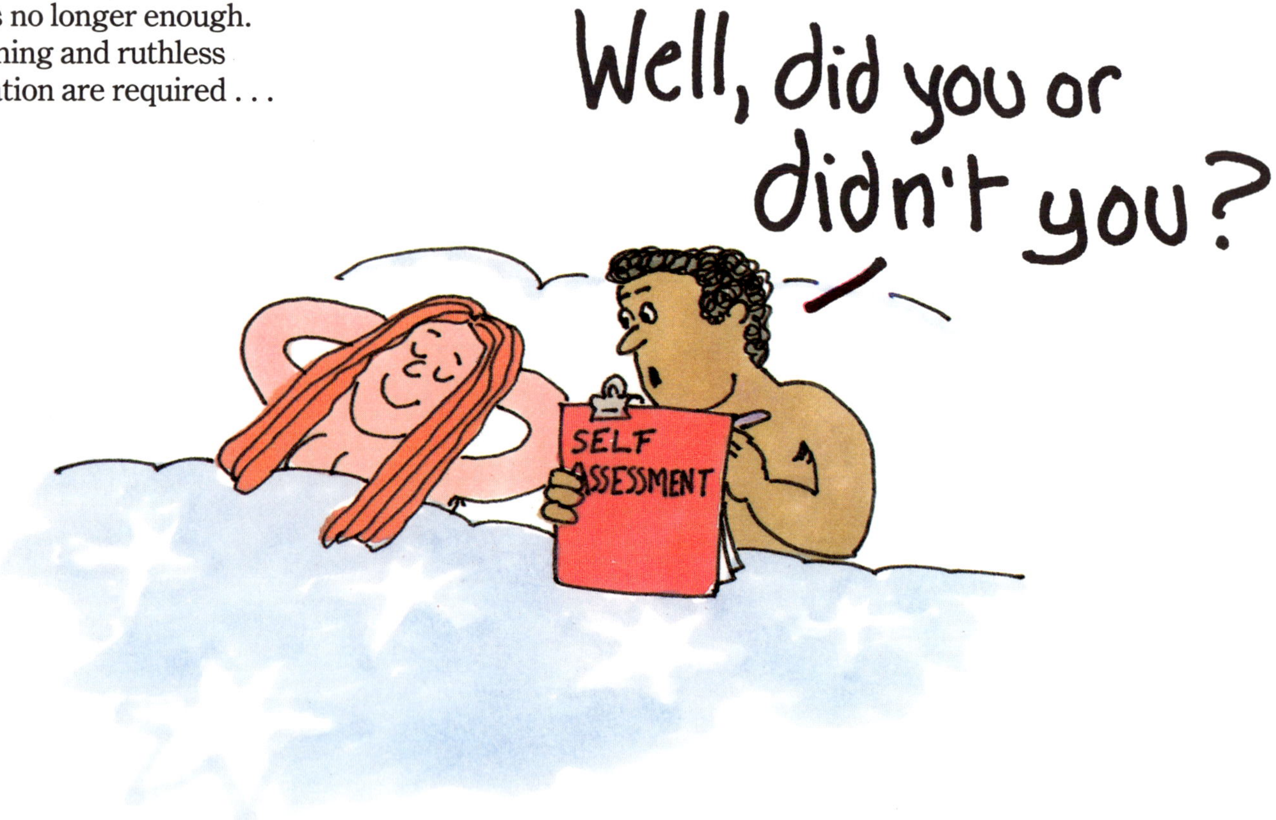
Well, did you or didn't you?
SELF ASSESSMENT

*BIG O – orgasm – eclipse of sun, earthquake, possibly some crashing waves in the distance.

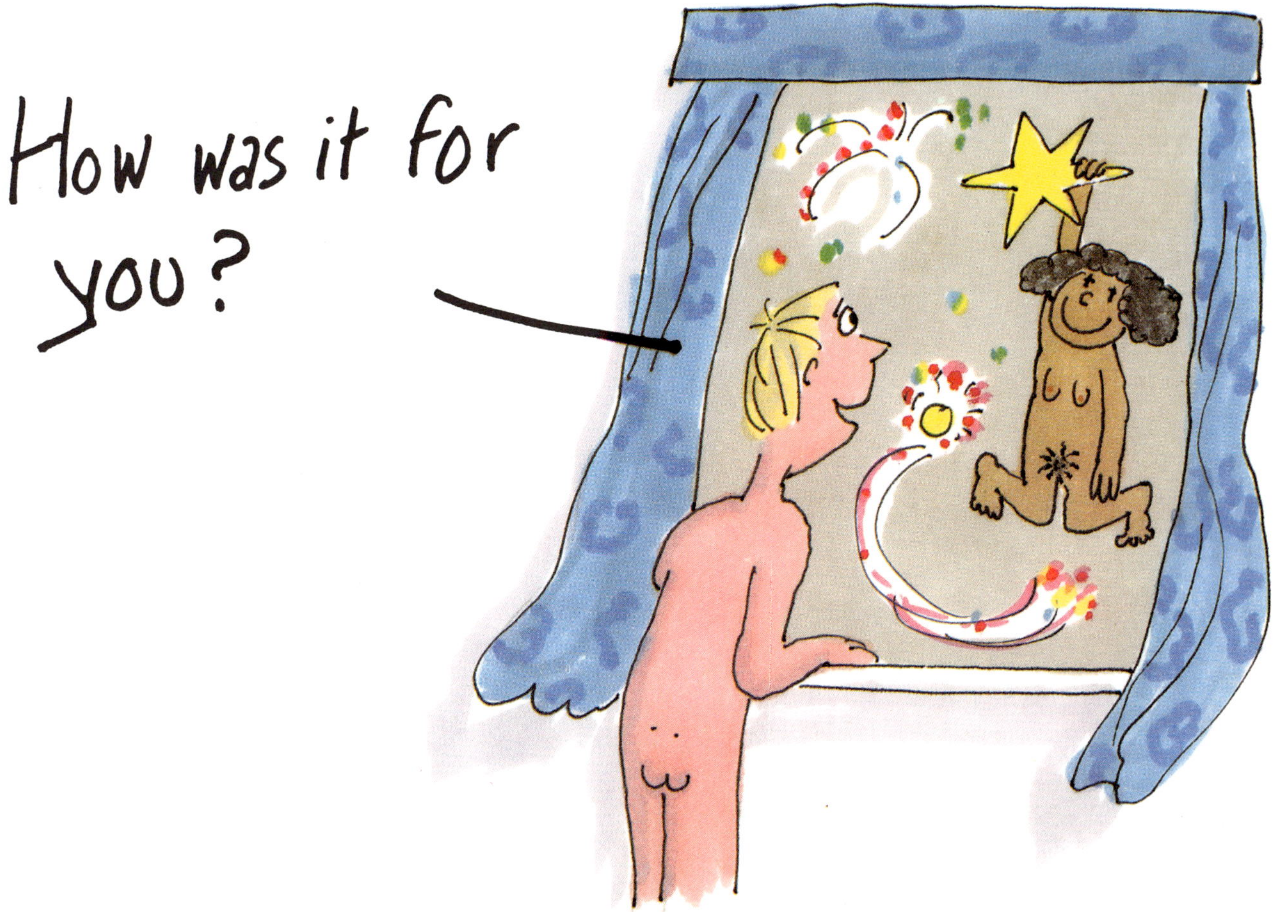
How was it for you?

SEXUAL CHEMISTRY . . .

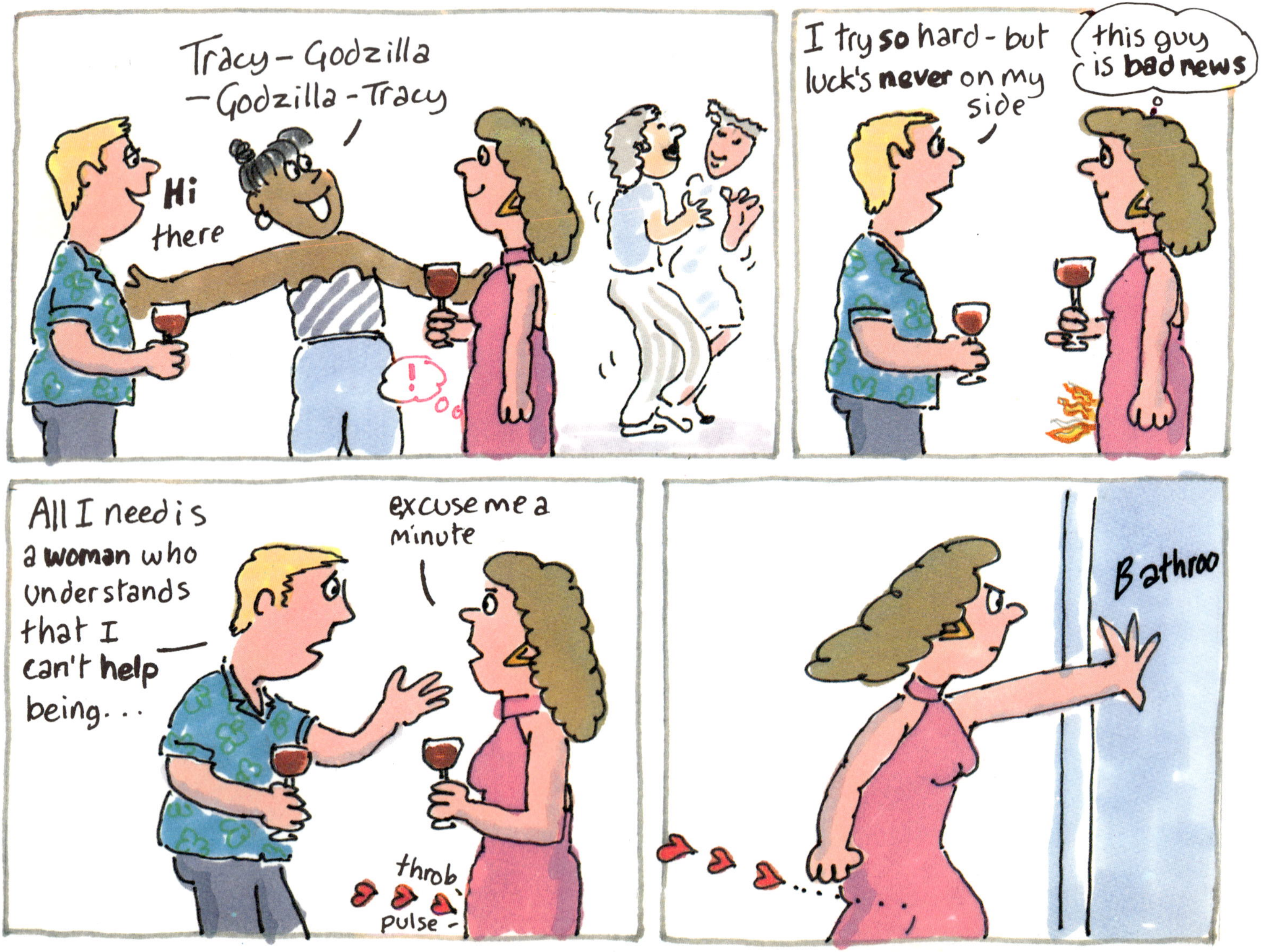
Tracy – Godzilla
– Godzilla – Tracy
Hi there
!
I try so hard – but luck's never on my side
this guy is bad news
All I need is a woman who understands that I can't help being . . .
excuse me a minute
throb
pulse –
Bathroo

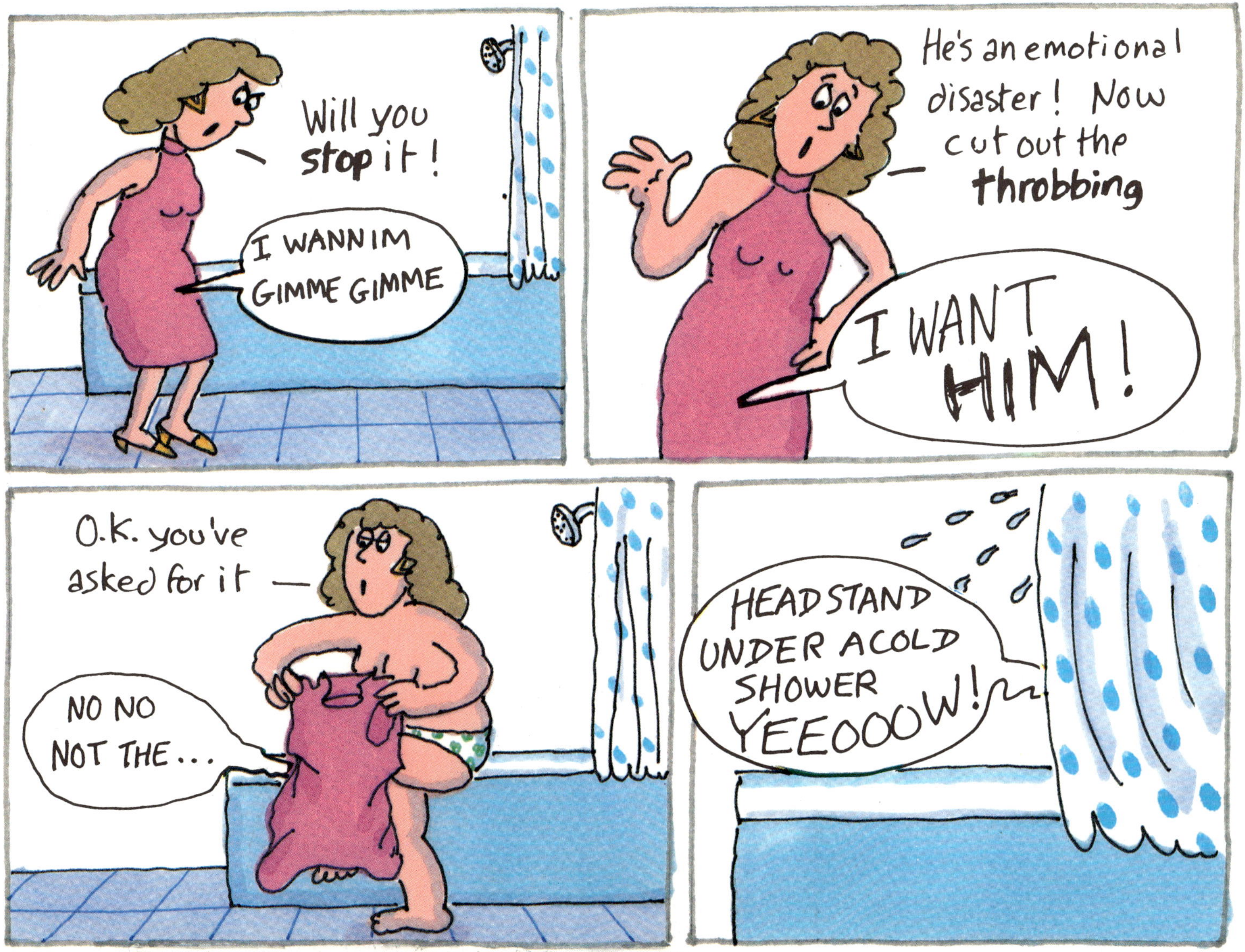

Will you stop it!
I WANNIM GIMME GIMME
He's an emotional disaster! Now cut out the throbbing
I WANT HIM!
O.K. you've asked for it
NO NO NOT THE...
HEADSTAND UNDER ACOLD SHOWER YEEOOOW!

DALLYING DYKES

Lesbians are leaping out of their closets nowadays, which makes it a lot easier to know who to chat up, according to personal inclination.

This new frankness also shatters the myth that women instinctively know what to do with each other . . .

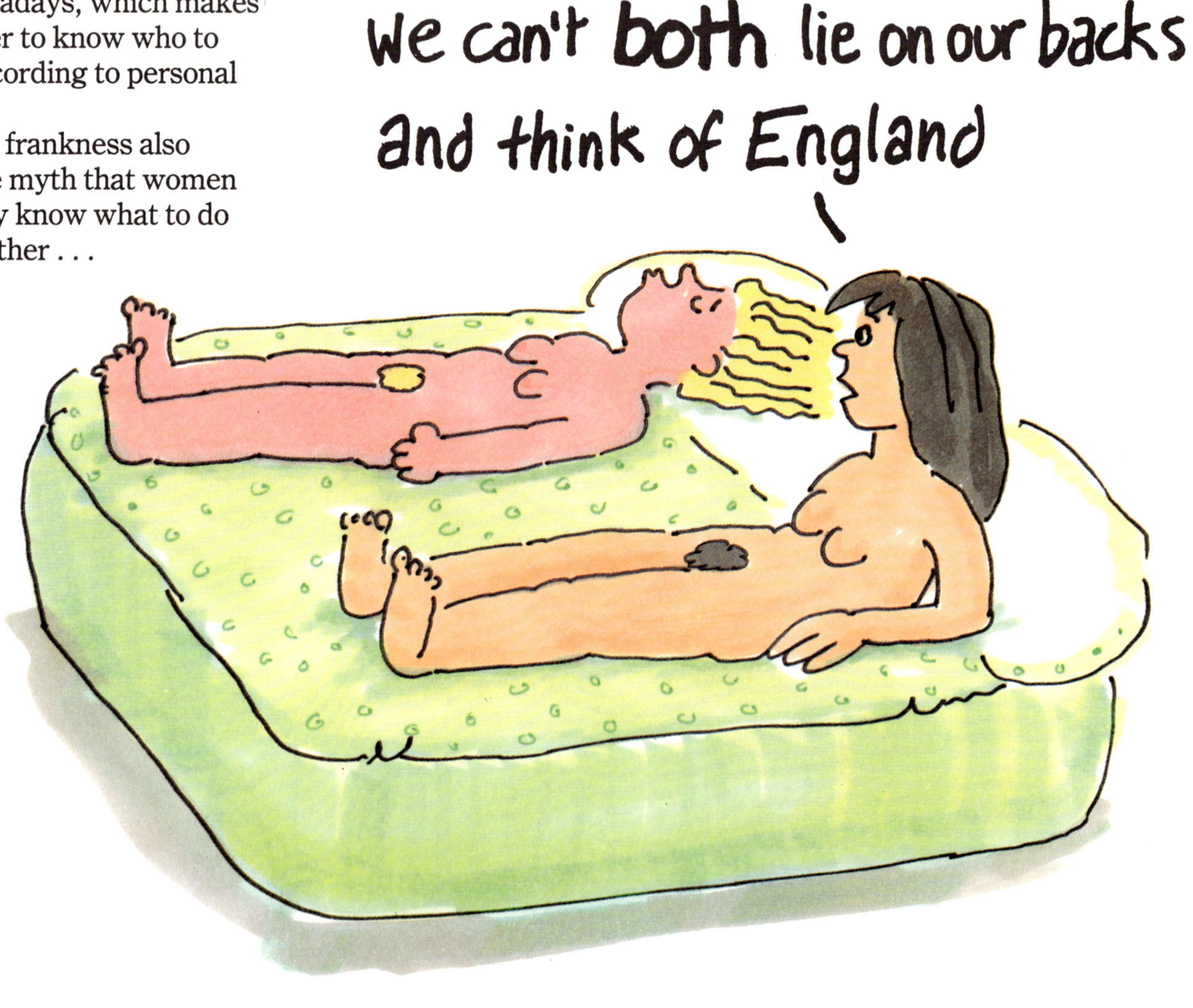
We can't both lie on our backs and think of England

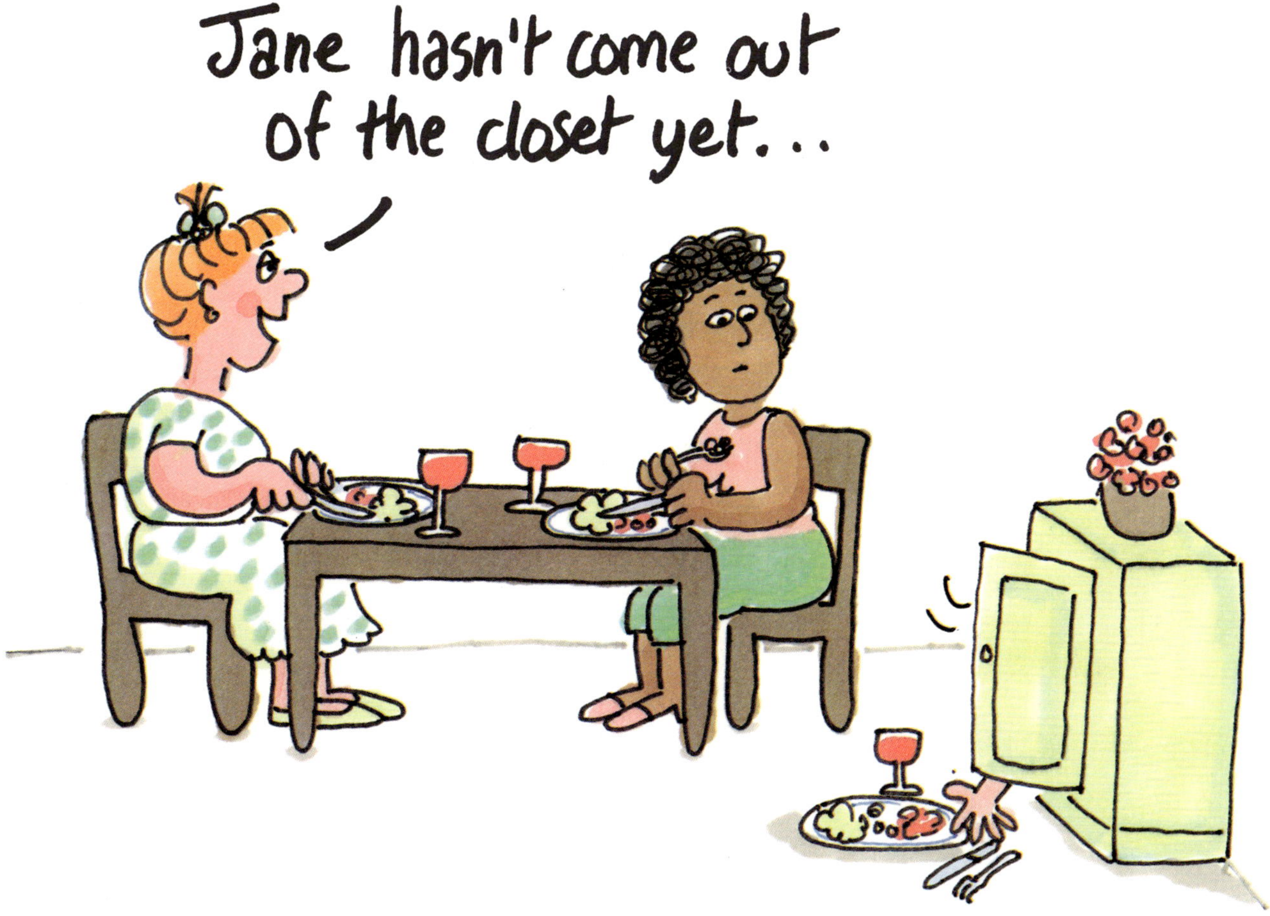
Jane hasn't come out of the closet yet...

OLDER WOMEN

Despite popular belief, Vajees don't retire gracefully at thirty. In fact they often blossom into a ripe old age.

This may cause problems when male peers go into early retirement or eternal rest.

Social Services installed a lift for you Darling

OPTIONS FOR VENERABLE VAJEES

Women, younger men, or for the
do-it-yourself cuddler, the hot
water bottle.

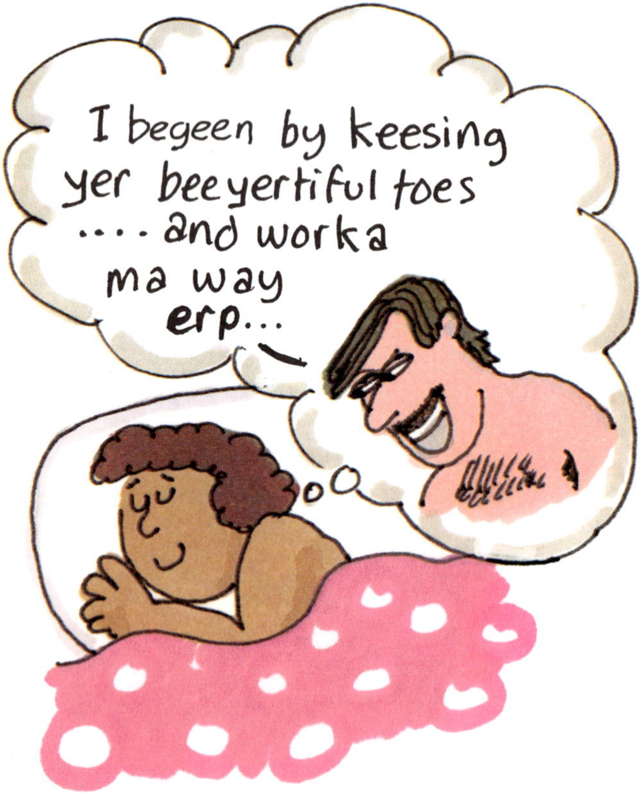
I begeen by keesing yer beeyertiful toes .... and worka ma way erp...

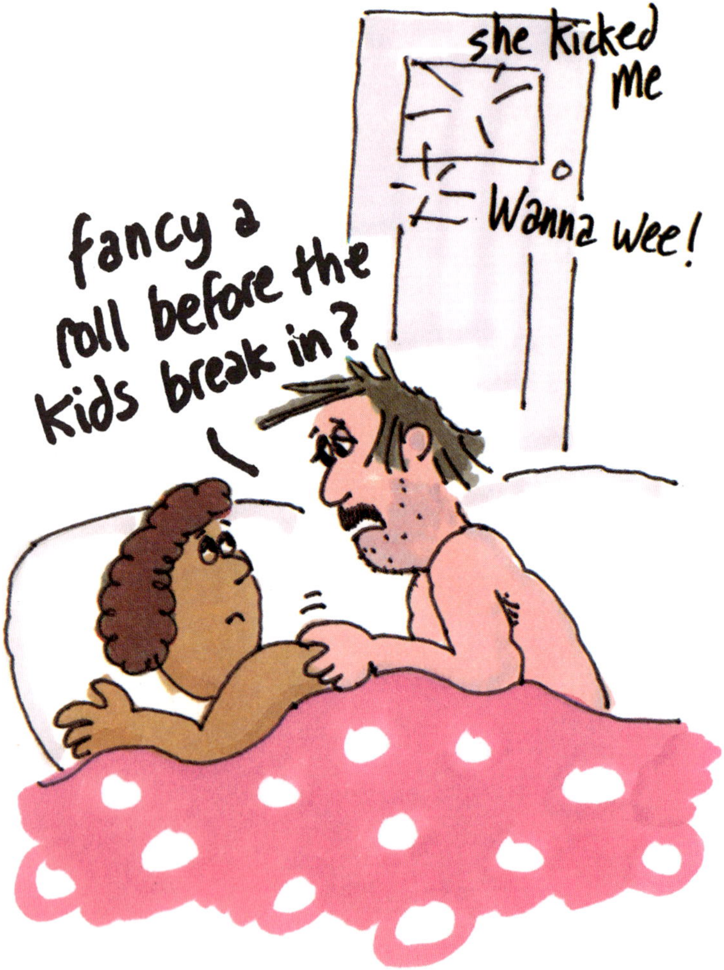
she kicked me
Wanna wee!
fancy a roll before the kids break in?

PETS

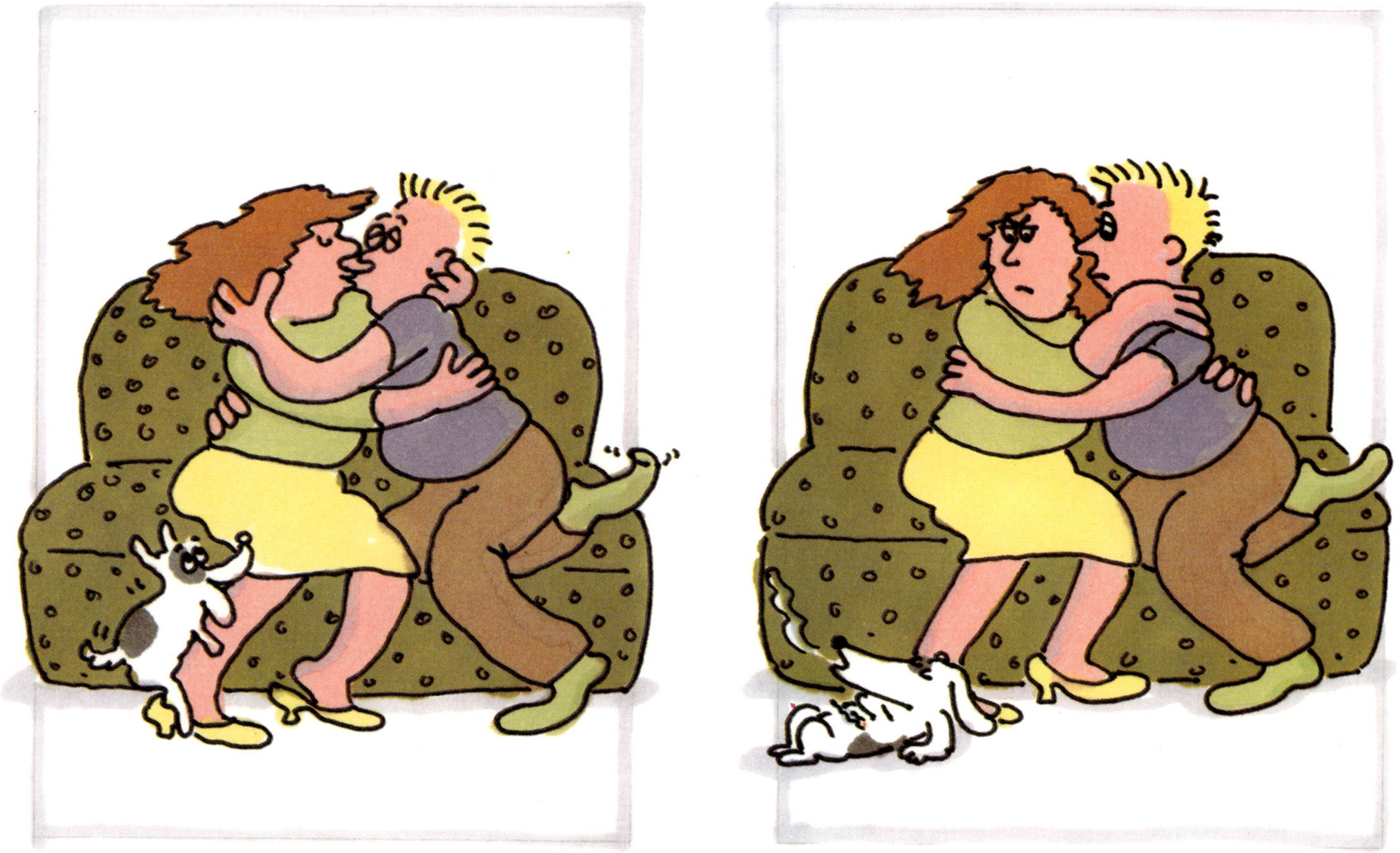

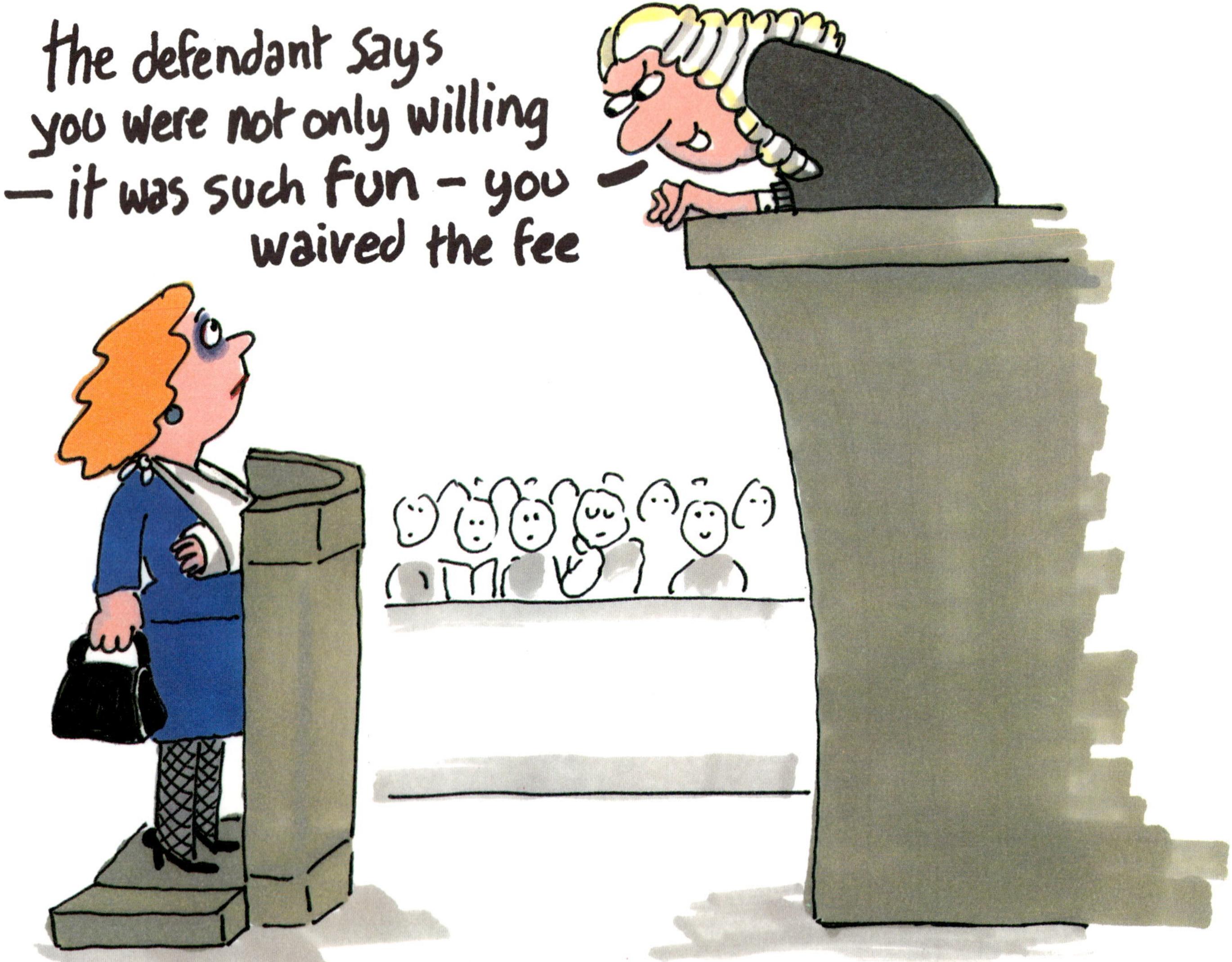
the defendant says you were not only willing – it was such fun – you waived the fee

VAJEE AS A BREAD WINNER

No qualifications or training necessary, cash on the nail, and you can work flexi-hours from home if you've got kids.

The perfect job for school leavers and mums! No sick pay, pension or security (but that's normal for women's work).

The only snag is, you can be sent to prison for selling what's yours . . . and the person buying it, gets let off.

Well, that's life isn't it?

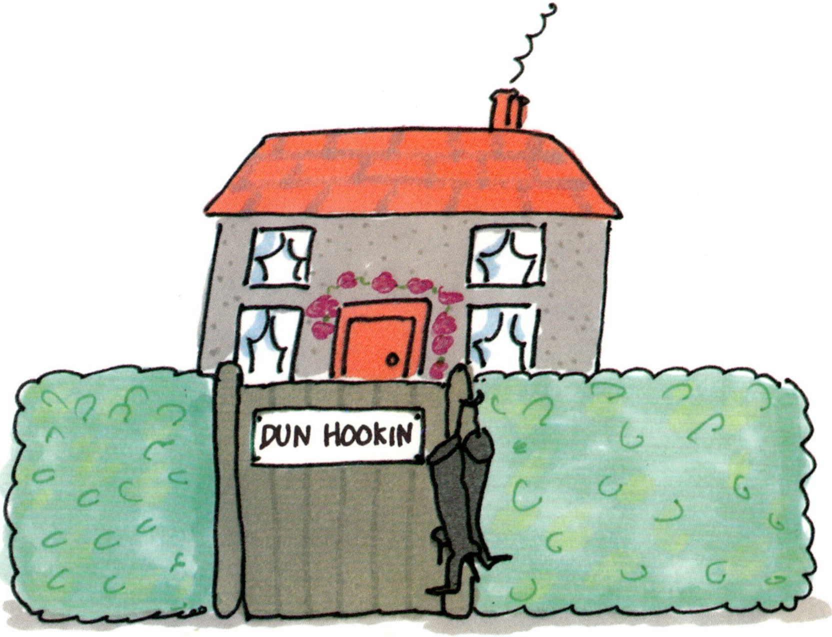
DUN HOOKIN

Fresh air freaks . . .

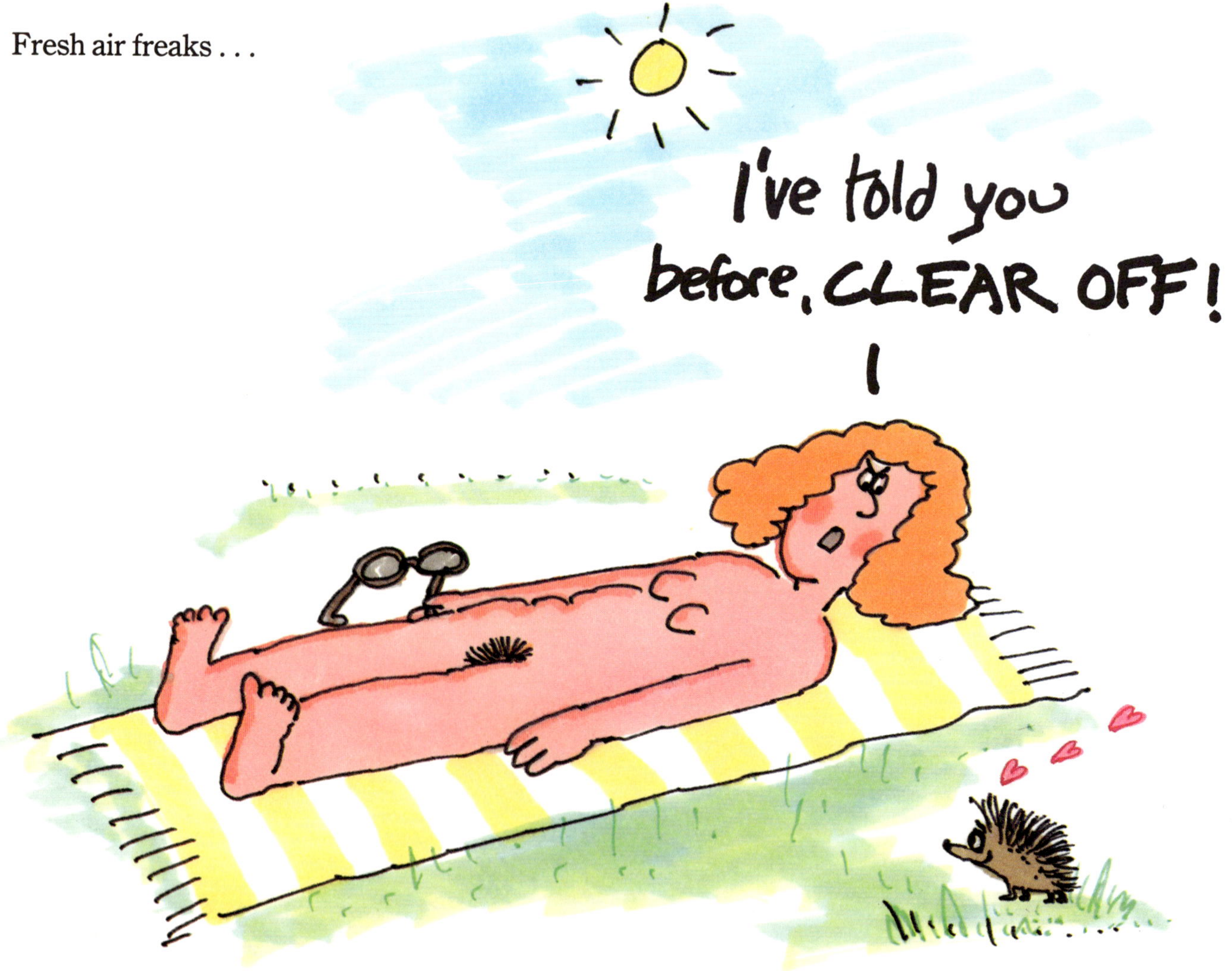

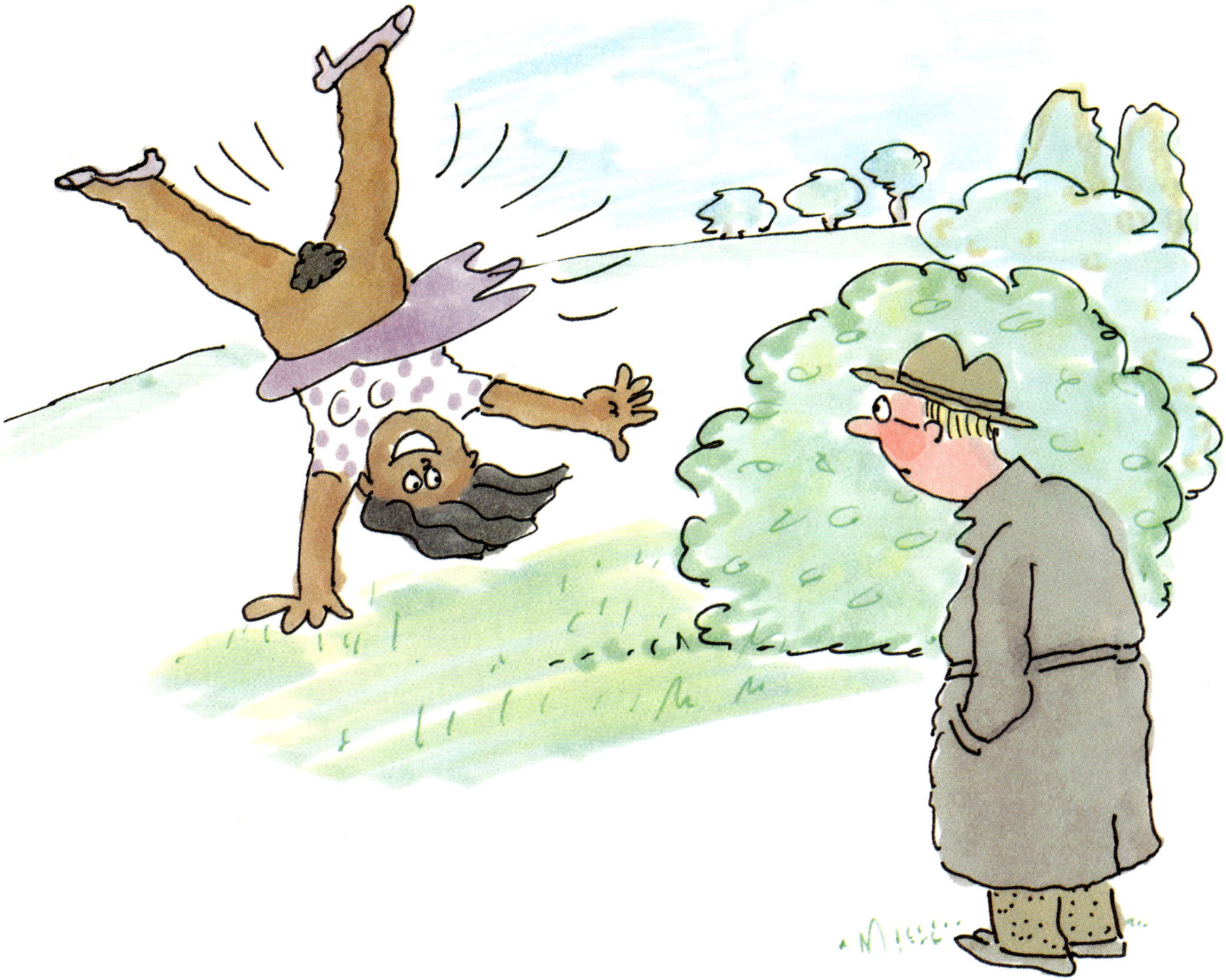

. . . and flashers

THE RELUCTANT VAJEE

Often caused by the *Double Standard* i.e. men gain reputations for Being Sexually Active. Women lose theirs for B.S.A.

Cures include signing the Official Secrets Act beforehand or wearing a tattooed sign on the forehead deploring double standards.

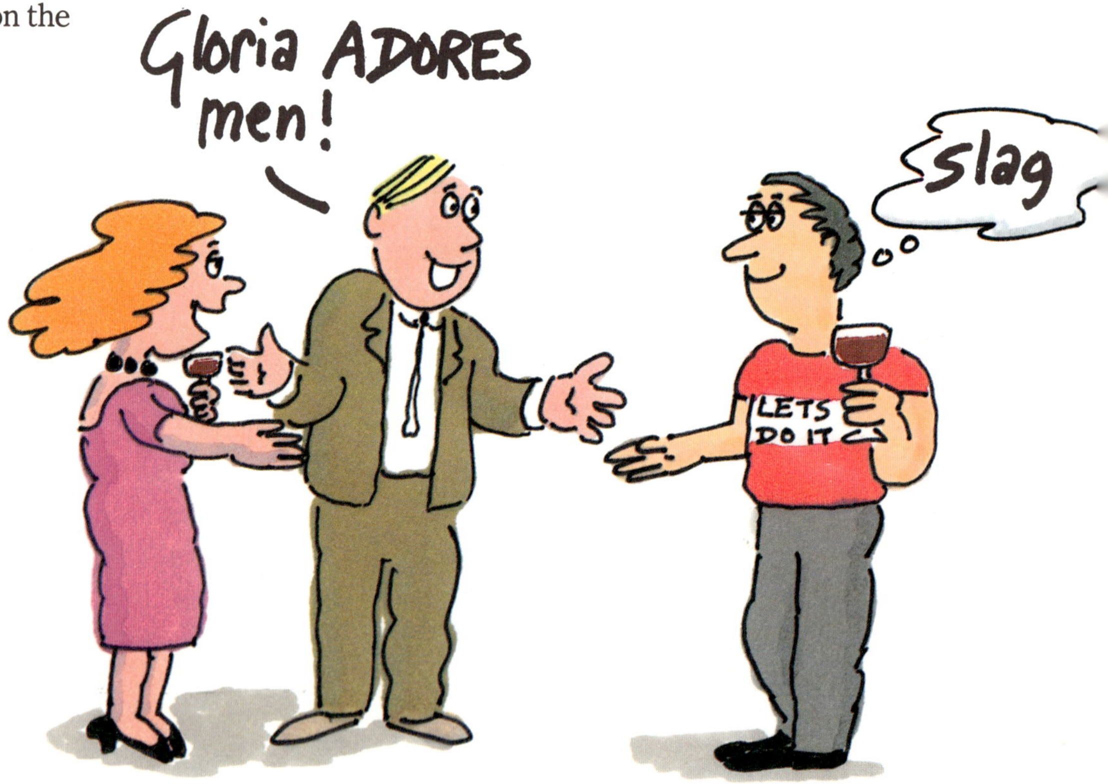
Gloria ADORES men!
slag
LETS DO IT

NO-GO AREAS

It's OK if you are married to God, but otherwise celibates commit the unpardonable sin of *not doing it at all.*

They often try to disguise this socially unacceptable way of life by hanging open-crotch knickers on the washing line to impress the neighbours.

must get back - she refuses to go to sleep til we've had at least five multiple orgasms

We're celibate

GIANT STEPS FOR WOMANKIND

Often occur when a man walks out and she has to cope on her own . . .

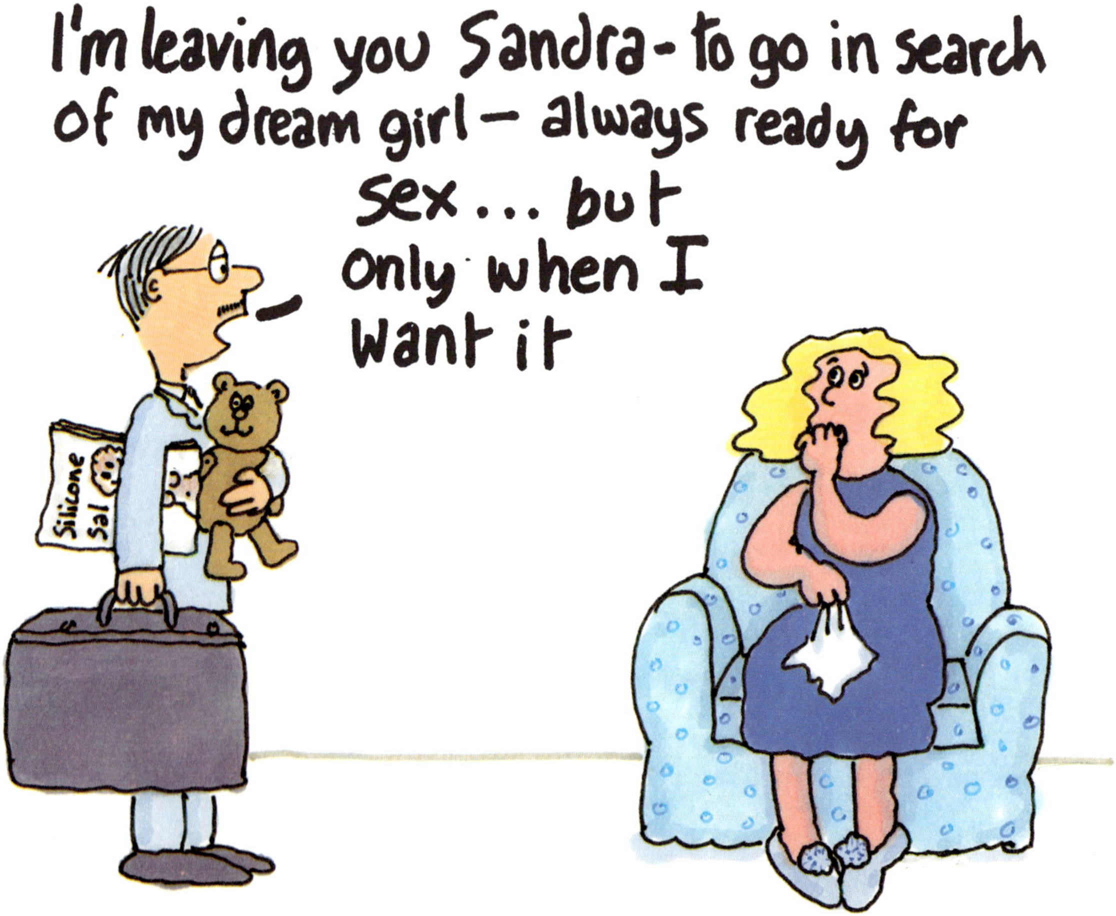
I'm leaving you Sandra - to go in search of my dream girl - always ready for sex ... but only when I want it
Silicone Sal

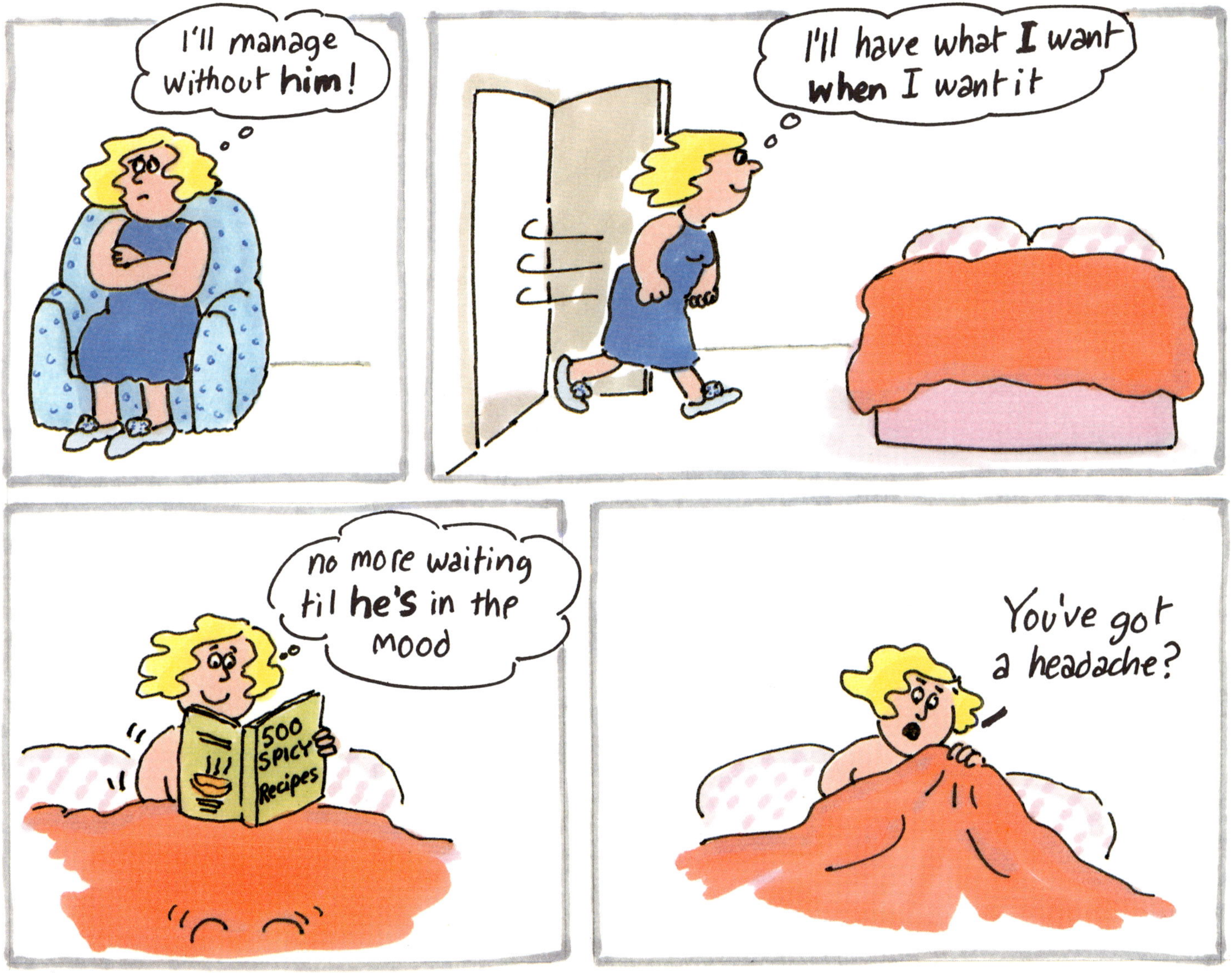
I'll manage without him!
I'll have what I want when I want it
no more waiting til he's in the mood
500 SPICY Recipes
You've got a headache?

THE TRAGEDY OF THE SOLAR-POWERED VIBRATOR

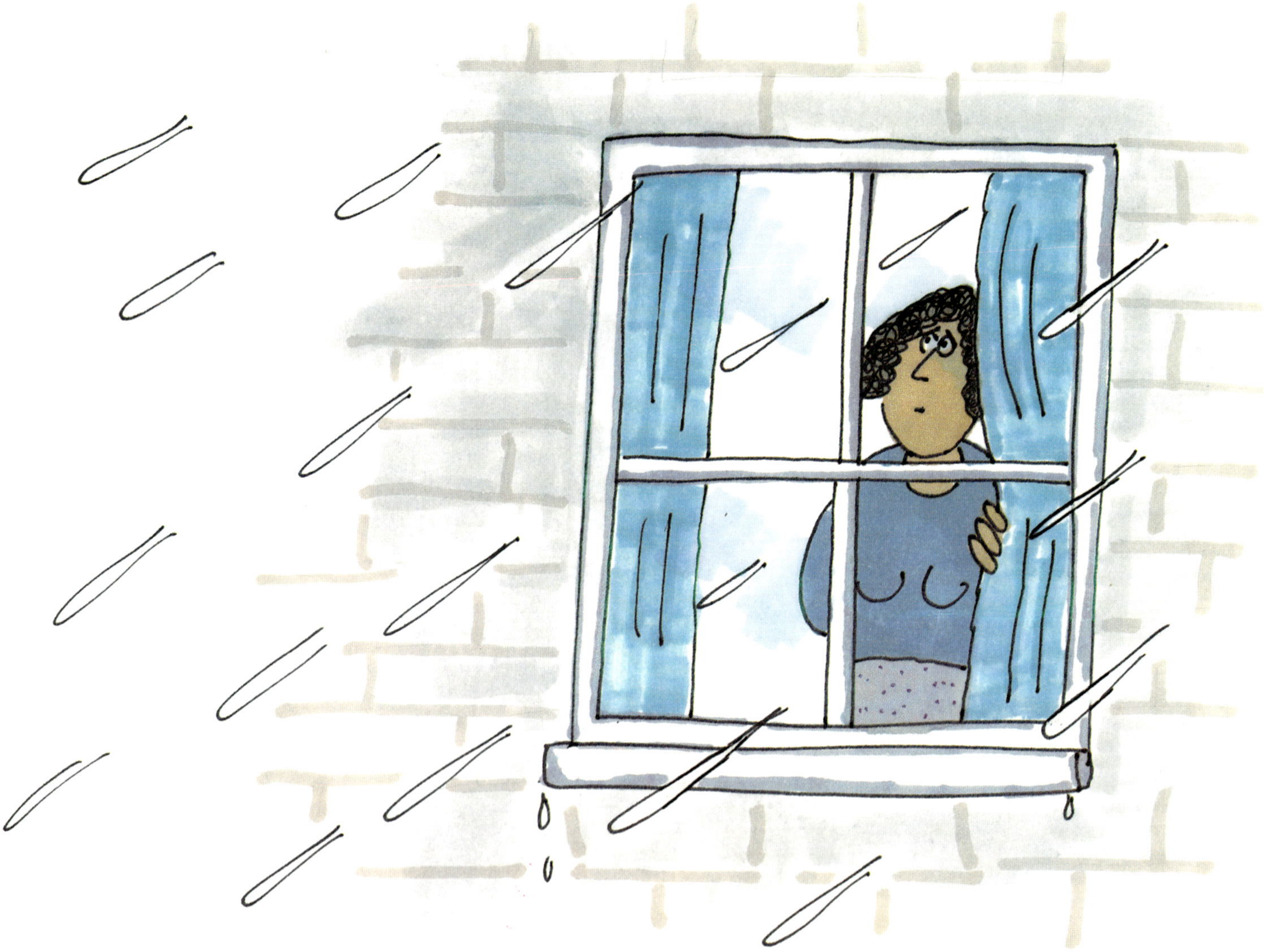

all on your own - night after night,
what do you DO with yourself Mother?

THE LONE LIBIDO

The main disadvantage is putting up with the pity heaped on you by those suffering from herpes, V.D., genital warts, etc. Advantages include:

- not suffering from herpes, V.D., genital warts, etc.

- not having to assist others in their weird perverted sexual practices

- being free to enjoy your own funny little habits – like having an affair with the corner of the spin dryer (the poor woman's vibrator).

HYGIENE

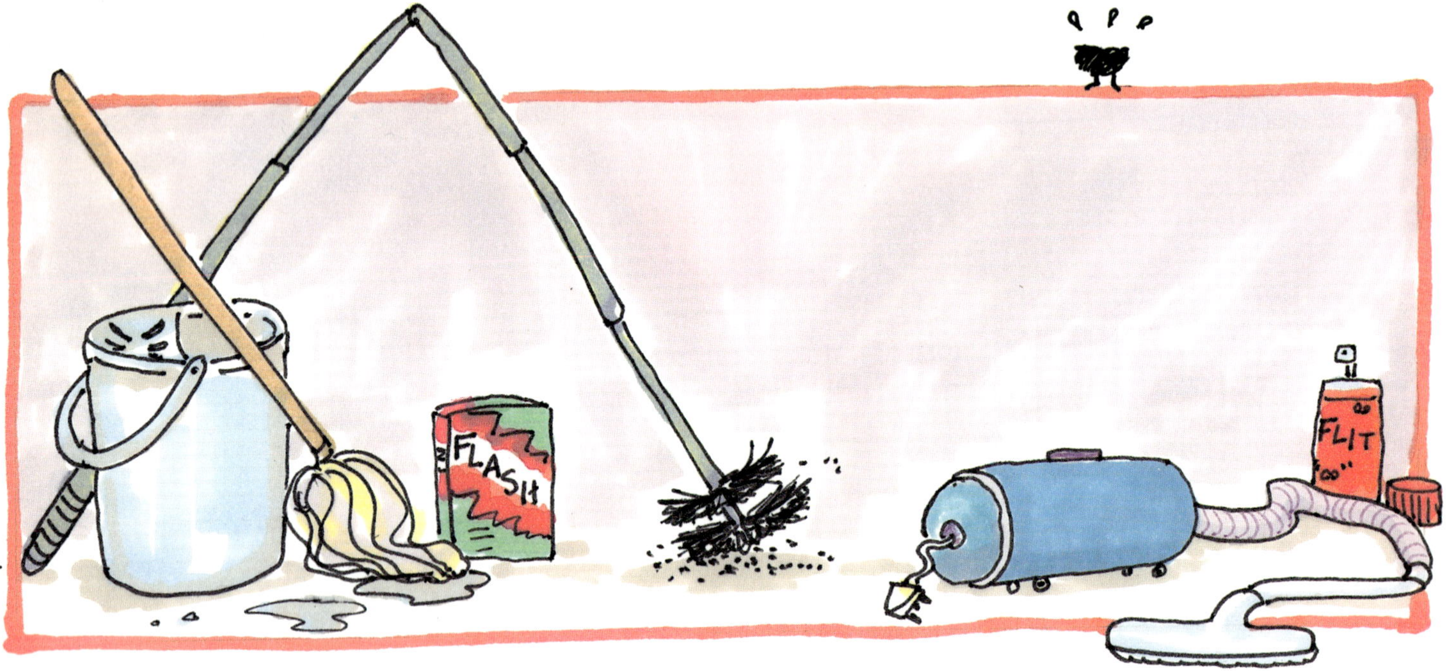
FLASH
FLIT

This equipment is rarely necessary in maintaining a hygienic Vajee. Her self-cleansing system does a very good job.

The main cause of germs comes from visitors . . .

WATCH OUT FOR . . . THE ONE-EYED TROUSER DOG

Also known as Man's Best Friend. Sticks its nose into anything and everything. Spreads germs faster than you can say 'V.D. clinic'.

Disinfect these chaps by soaking overnight in biological detergent. Then steam wrap in a double layer of cling film before allowing entry.

AIDS

For the woman who enjoys putting herself about, times have never been so hard . . .

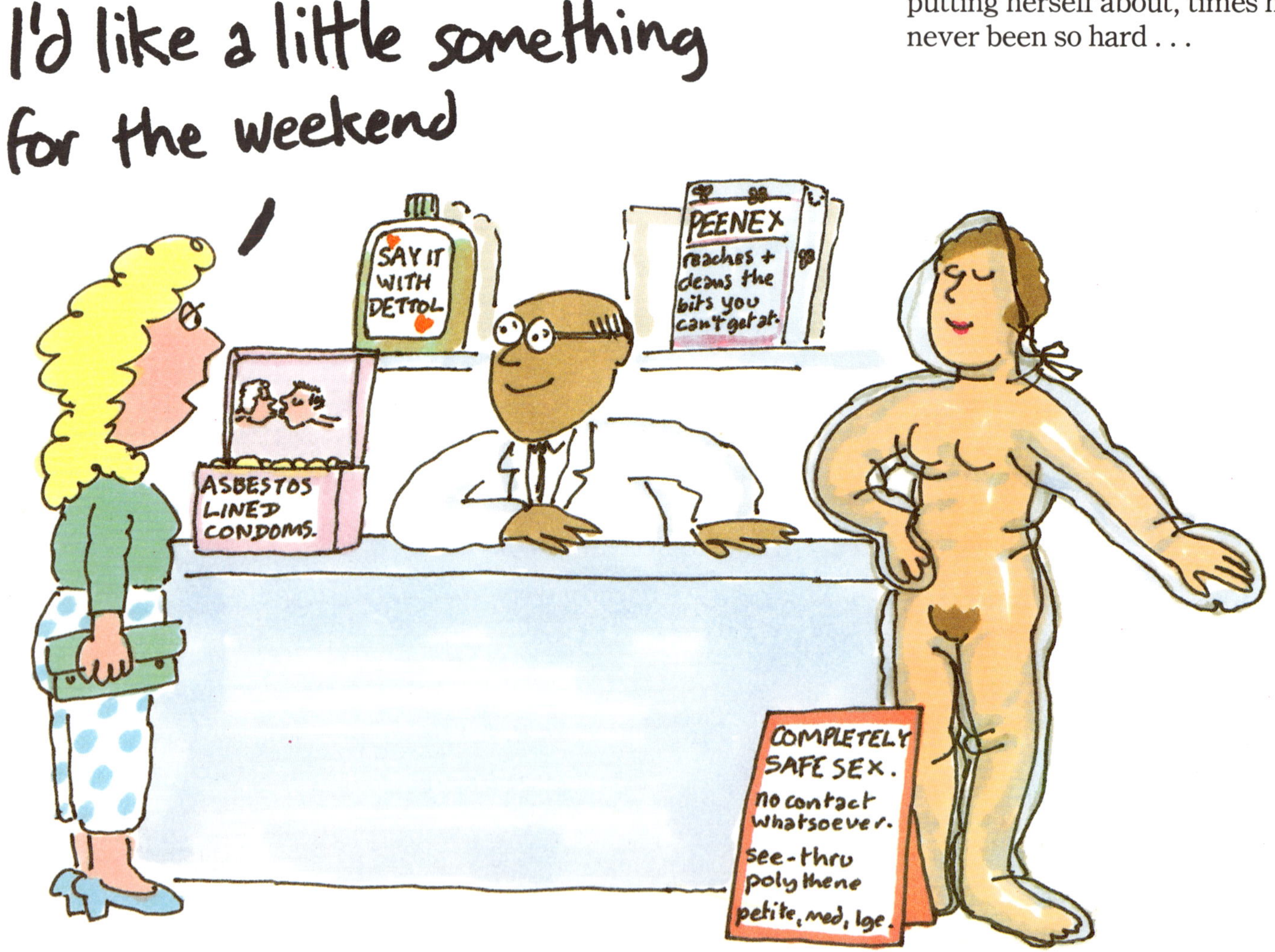
I'd like a little something for the weekend
SAY IT WITH DETTOL
PEENEX
reaches + cleans the bits you can't get at.
ASBESTOS LINED CONDOMS.
COMPLETELY SAFE SEX.
no contact whatsoever.
see-thru polythene
petite, med, lge.

NYMPHOMANIAC

- a woman who has had as many affairs as the man who called her a nymphomaniac.
- a woman who wants sex when her partner isn't in the mood.

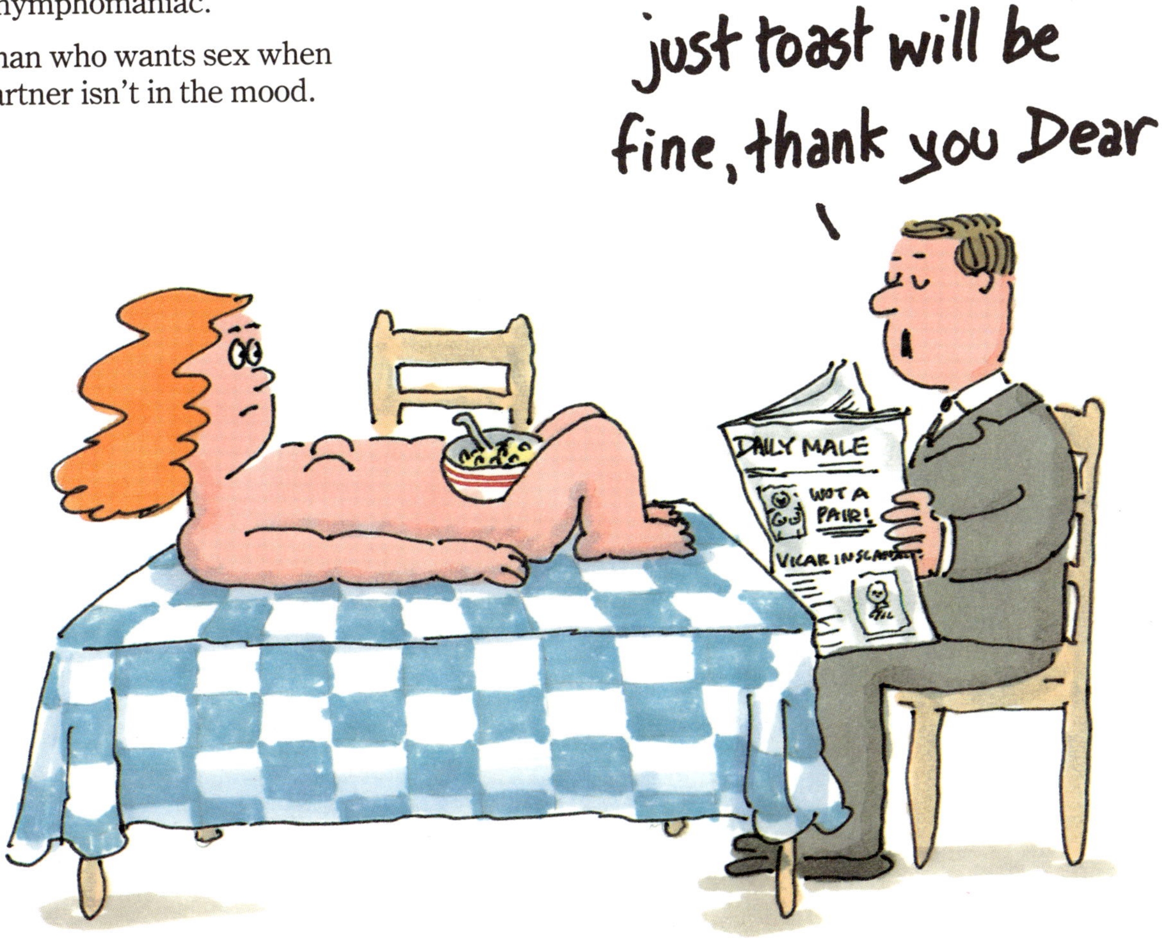
just toast will be fine, thank you Dear
DAILY MALE
WOT A PAIR!

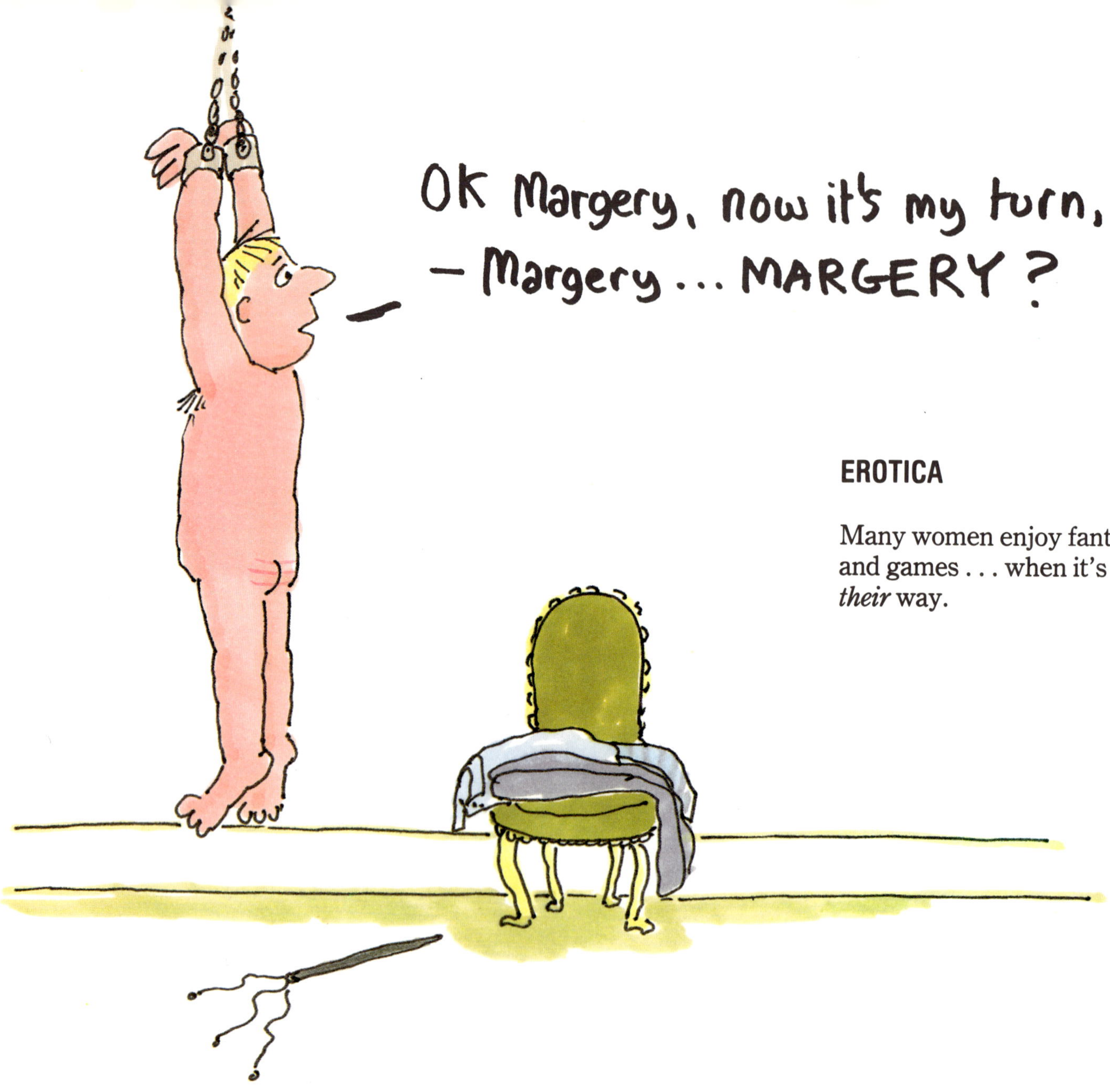
OK Margery, now it's my turn,
– Margery ... MARGERY ?

EROTICA

Many women enjoy fantasies and games . . . when it's done *their* way.

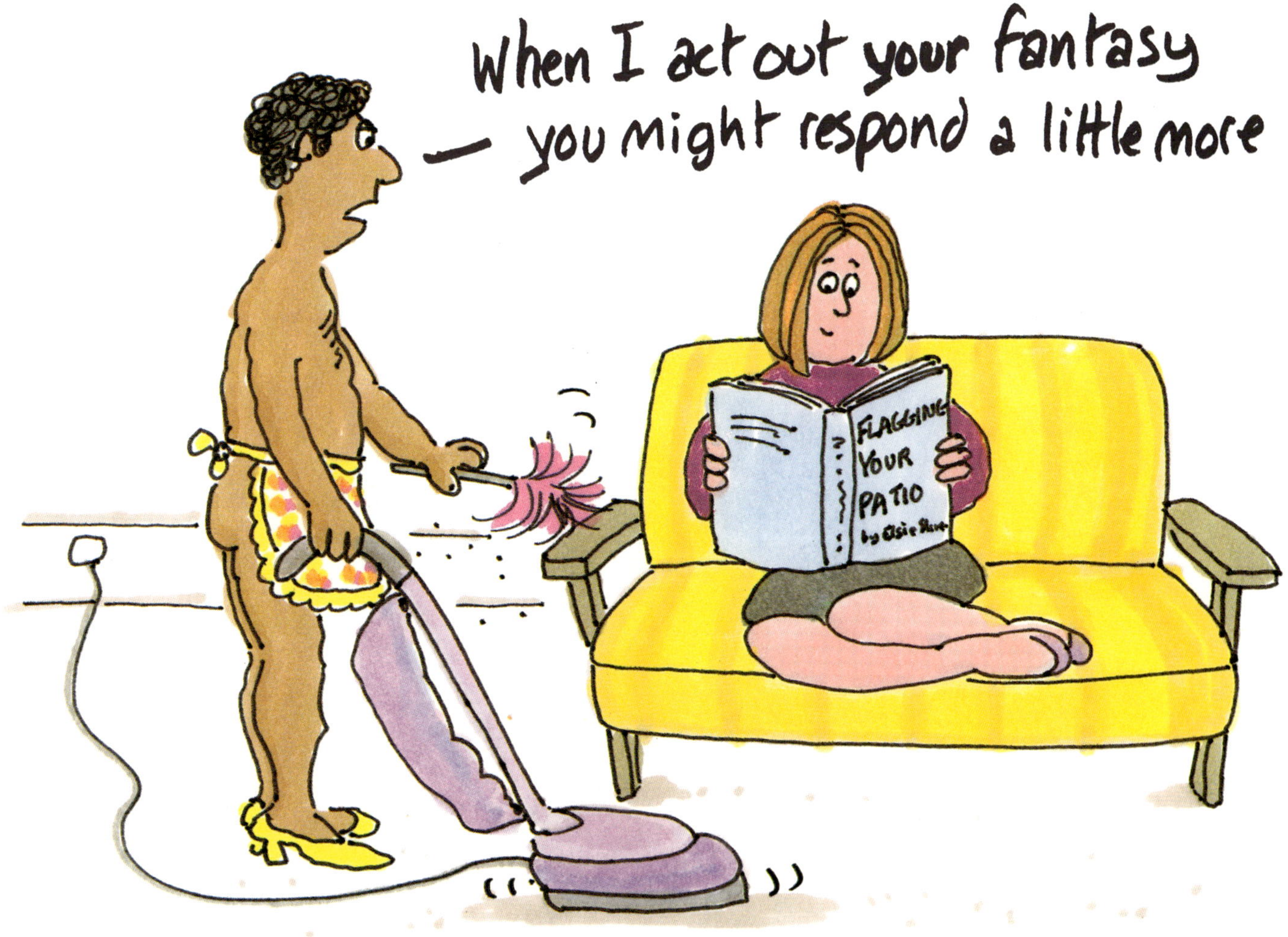
When I act out your fantasy — you might respond a little more
FLAGGING YOUR PATIO

KNOWING WHAT YOU WANT

(getting it is something else)

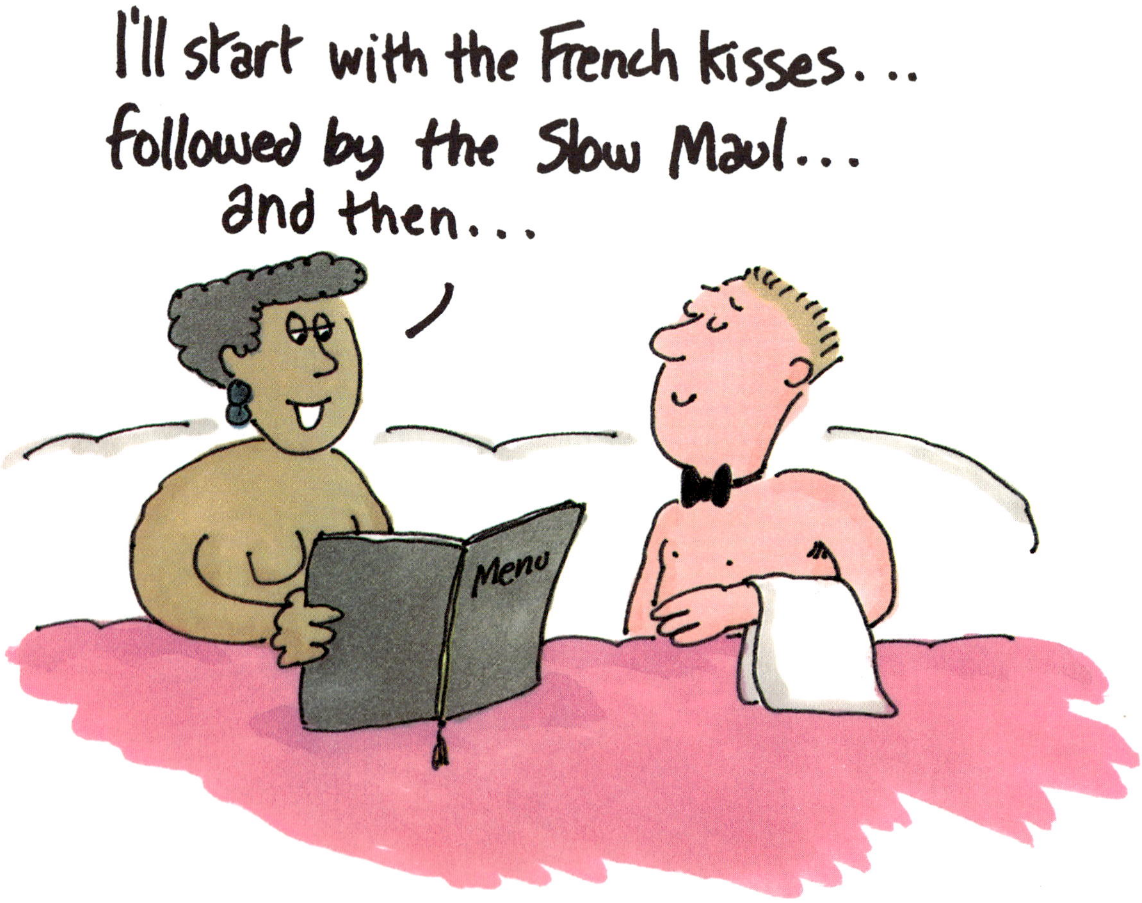
I'll start with the French kisses...
followed by the Slow Maul...
and then...
Menu

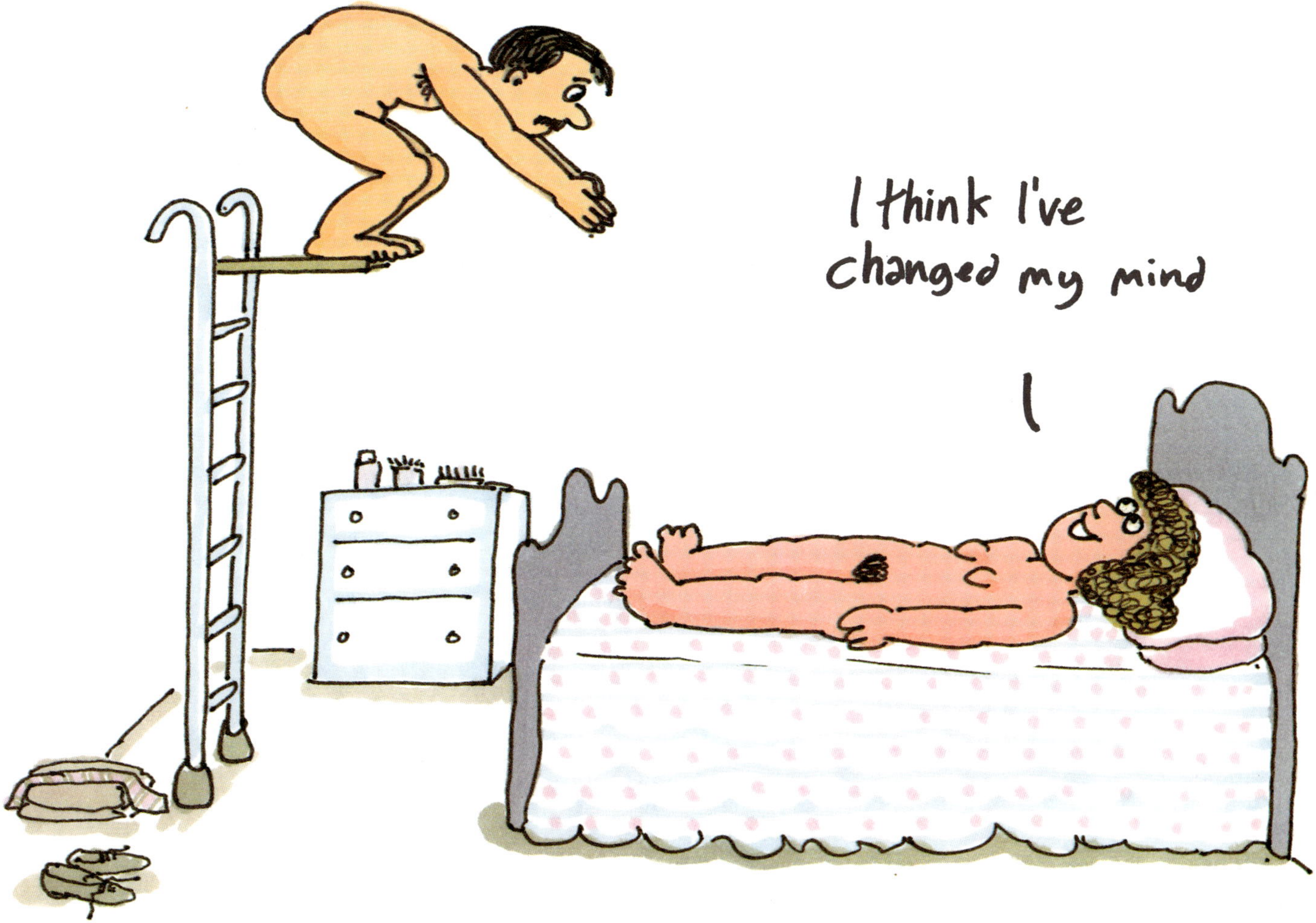
I think I've changed my mind

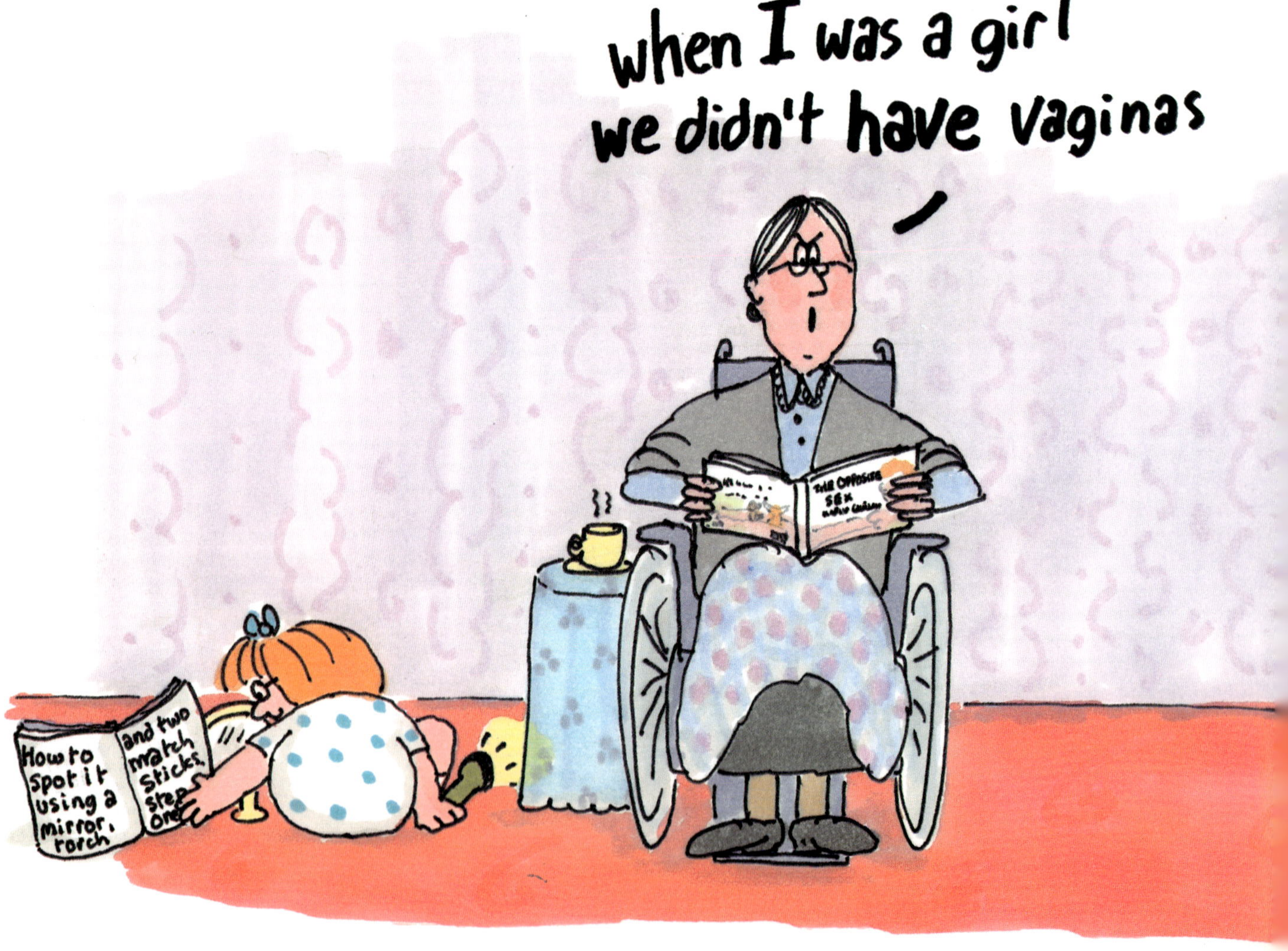
when I was a girl we didn't have vaginas
THE OPPOSITE SEX
How to spot it using a mirror, torch
and two match sticks. step one

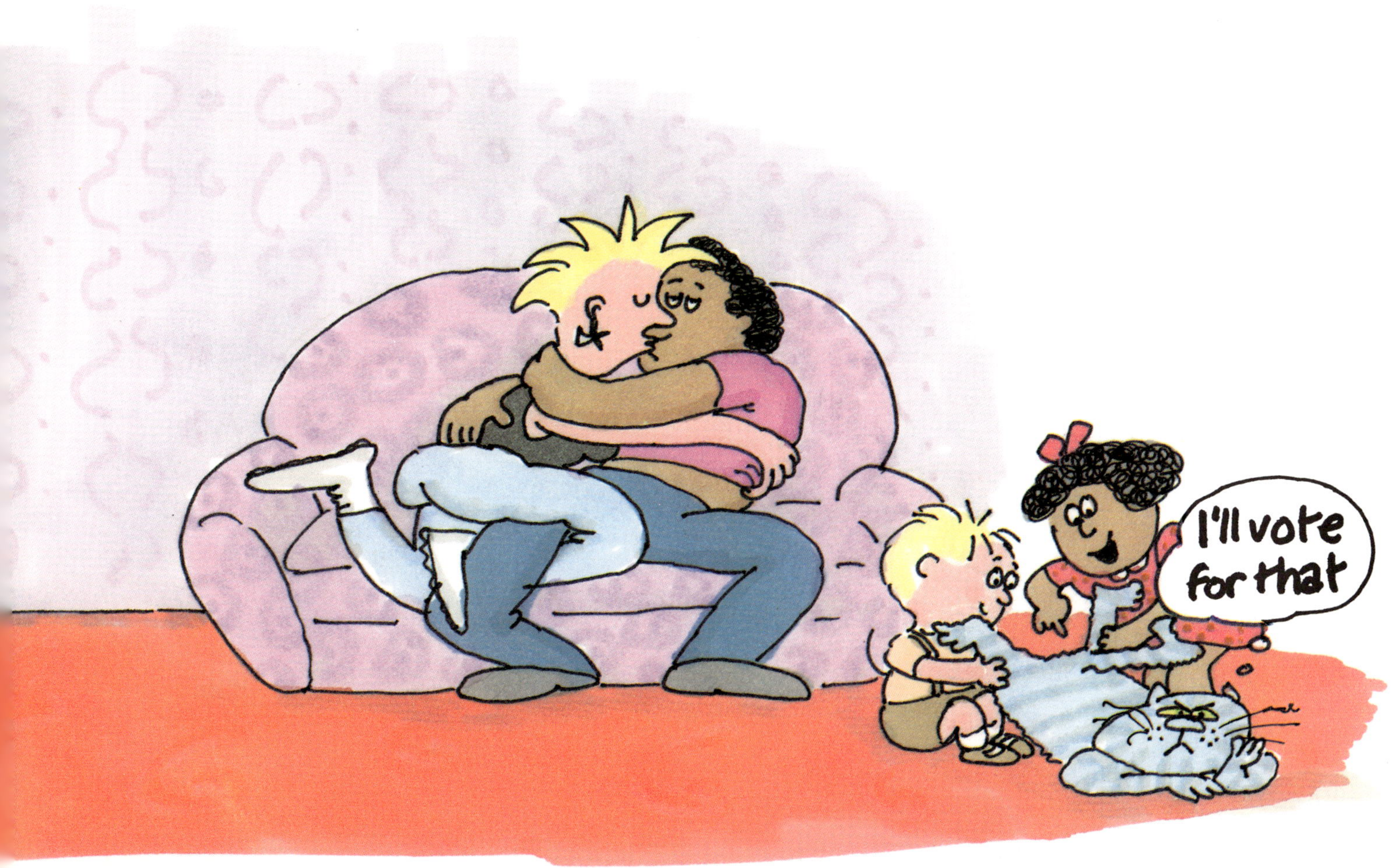
I'll vote for that

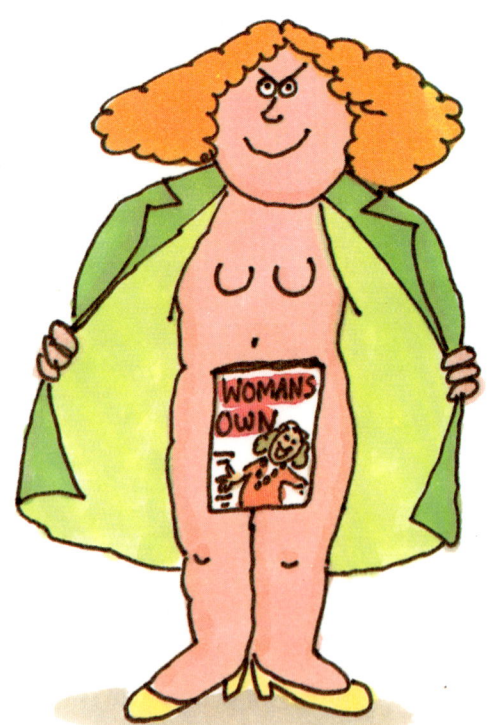

Grafton Books
A Division of the Collins Publishing Group
8 Grafton Street, London W1X 3LA

A Grafton Paperback Original 1987

Copyright © Viv Quillin 1987

ISBN 0-586-07425-2

Printed and bound in Great Britain by
Collins, Glasgow

Set in Century Old Style and Helios